Ken Follett

Ken Follett:
The Transformation of a Writer

Carlos Ramet

Bowling Green State University Popular Press
Bowling Green, OH 43403

Copyright 1999 © Bowling Green State University Popular Press

Library of Congress Cataloging-in-Publication Data
Ramet, Carlos.
      Ken Follett : the transformation of a writer / Carlos Ramet.
          p.   cm.
      Includes bibliographical references (p.   ) and index.
      ISBN 0-87972-797-7 (clothbound). -- ISBN 0-87972-798-5 (pbk.)
      1. Follett, Ken--Criticism and interpretation.   I. Title.
   PR6056.045Z76   1999
   823'.914--dc21
                                                      99-21431
                                                         CIP

Cover design by Dumm Art

To Jean

CONTENTS

ACKNOWLEDGEMENTS

I would like to thank the anonymous participants at the seminars and conferences at which very early drafts of these chapters were first presented, as well as the editors and readers of those journals which have published versions of those conference papers. All of their comments have been useful in the revision process.

A version of chapter 1 was first presented at the Popular Culture Association Conference in Louisville, Kentucky, in March 1992 under the title "Ken Follett and the Decline of the West" and was published as "Ken Follett from Start to Finish: The Transformation of a Writer" in *Studies in Popular Culture* 15.2 (1993): 79-86.

Chapter 2 was originally given as a paper at the Popular Culture Association Conference, in New Orleans, Louisiana, in April 1993.

Chapter 3 was first presented as a paper at the Popular Culture Association Conference held in Las Vegas, Nevada, in March 1996.

Chapter 4 was given at the Michigan Academy of Science, Arts and Letters Annual Conference held in Grand Rapids, Michigan, in March 1997 and was later published under the title "Reinvigorating the Thriller: Ken Follett's *Eye of the Needle* as Literature." The article appeared in *The Michigan Academician* 30.4 (1998): 387-97.

A draft of Chapter 5 was presented under the title "From Fiction to Film: Artistic Transmutation in Ken Follett's *Eye of the Needle*" at the Michigan Academy of Science, Arts and Letters Annual Conference, held in East Lansing, Michigan, in March 1994.

Chapter 6 was presented under the title "Follett on Film: The Key to *The Key to Rebecca*" at the Popular Culture Association Conference in Chicago, Illinois, in April 1994.

Chapter 7 was first given at the Mid-Atlantic Popular Culture Conference held in Philadelphia, Pennsylvania, in November 1996.

Chapter 8 was originally presented at the Popular Culture Association Conference in New Orleans, Louisiana, in March 1988, and was published by *Clues: A Journal of Detection* Vol. 9.2 (1988): 63-73.

Chapter 9 was given at the Mid-West Popular Culture Association Conference held in Pittsburgh, Pennsylvania, in October 1994, and was published in the *Popular Culture Review* 7.2 (1996): 135-43.

Chapter 10 was originally given under the title "Politics and the Historical Novel: Ken Follett as Revisionist" at the Mid-West Popular

Culture Association Conference in Indianapolis, Indiana, in November 1995.

A number of institutions and individuals also deserve recognition. I would like to thank the University of Illinois-Chicago for its foresight in offering graduate-level courses in Popular Culture Theory and in particular would like to mention Dr. John Huntington, whose classes provided a foundation and piqued an early interest in the author who would become the subject of this book. Professor James Park Sloan furnished equal encouragement and taught me the importance of writing and publishing fiction before attempting to critique it.

The Popular Culture Association has provided countless opportunities for scholars at all stages of their careers. The conferences organized by Ray and Pat Browne have been a forum for the discussion of many of the ideas in this text; Pat Browne's early interest in my work and publication of a first article encouraged me to continue with this project; I also owe a debt of gratitude to the editorial and production staff of Popular Press.

My home institution, Saginaw Valley State University, has generously allowed me to pursue my teaching and research interests in a number of ways: opportunities to teach Popular Culture and British Literature have resulted in the fresh input from my students; professional development funding has made travel and conference attendance feasible; a winter 1998 sabbatical allowed for the completion of this text. I am particularly grateful for the encouragement of Drs. Judith Kerman and Donald J. Bachand who, while serving as Dean of the College, have helped provide such support. I would also like to thank the Vice President for Academic Affairs, Dr. Robert S. P. Yien, who made possible extended research at the University of Michigan and at Michigan State University.

My agent of long-standing, Dr. Barbara Bauer of the Barbara Bauer Literary Agency, has provided considerable encouragement over the years as well as professional advice.

Thanks also to my friend and colleague, Dr. Paul Munn, for graciously agreeing to read page proofs.

Clearly, many people have contributed to the evolution of this volume, not the least of whom has been my wife, who understood the direction these various articles and papers were taking well before I did. Her belief in me and in the value of this project has been of great comfort. During a winter sabbatical, when much of this work was rewritten, she became my only audience. I must thank her for her forbearance and above all for establishing an atmosphere that was conducive to cheerful reflection.

ABBREVIATIONS

BR	*The Bear Raid*
DF	*A Dangerous Fortune*
HE	*The Hammer of Eden*
PC	*A Place Called Freedom*
PM	*Paper Money*
SK	*The Shakeout*
TT	*The Third Twin*

PREFACE

When the Welsh-born and working-class Ken Follett began writing mystery and detective stories in the early 1970s, the prevailing belief in university circles was that "virtually any piece of classical music or 'serious' work of fiction, no matter how undistinguished, was felt to be inherently more important" than the greatest example of popular culture.[1] In part, this dismissal of mass-market paperbacks and popular novels may have had to do with the intended audience for such works—lower-middle class and working-class readers.

The erosion over the past 25 years of this academic viewpoint toward the curriculum is well known: the leveling influence of semiotics, with its emphasis on the "signs" that make up language, and the anti-hierarchical stance of post-structuralism and reader-response theory have coincided with the development of popular culture criticism and an increased willingness among academics to undertake a serious scrutiny of what had previously been considered the routine throwaways of a society—mystery novels, spy stories, and historical romances.

Numerous scholars have pointed to the origins of these three genres in the conditions of early 19th-century life, with the relative extension of literacy and leisure time and the subsequent demand for reading as entertainment. One of the first fiction writers to benefit from these conditions and to approach literature almost exclusively as a trade was Sir Walter Scott, whose development of the historical romance and cultivation of a public following set a course for many subsequent writers, from James Fenimore Cooper through Edgar Allan Poe to Ken Follett. Follett, in fact, stands as both inheritor and amender of a certain popular tradition, and it is worth considering the literary antecedents that have allowed for his success.

Though some scholars have pointed to Homer's episode of the Trojan Horse as the precursor of all stories of subterfuge, or to Cooper's *The Spy* (1821) and Poe's "The Purloined Letter" (1845) as early examples of the story of international intrigue, the subcategory that formed the basis of Follett's youthful reading and became the genre for which he is best known—the British chase melodrama—finds its true origins in the "Fear of Invasion" novels prevalent at the end of the 19th century and after the Franco-Prussian war.

The first generation of British writers to capitalize upon popular anxieties about the end of "splendid isolation" and the horizon of world war would include William Le Queux, E. Phillips Oppenheim, Erskine Childers, John Buchan, and H. C. McNeile ("Sapper"), whose often deeply conservative adventure stories tended to triumph the values of the British public school—loyalty to class and caste, the importance of order and sportsmanship, and the indomitability of the plucky individual. To a certain extent, these patterns occur in Ken Follett's early spy novels, especially with their motifs of the alien invader in "little England" (*Eye of the Needle* [1978] and *The Man from St. Petersburg* [1982]), the chase for a secret device or document (*Triple* [1979], *The Key to Rebecca* [1980]), and the "Clubland" atmosphere of his two Piers Roper books (*The Shakeout* [1975], and *The Bear Raid* [1976]).

With the movement from the mere anticipation of political hostilities to a direct experience of wartime and interwar confrontation, a second generation of British spy writers added to and amended the genre. Influenced by Joseph Conrad's psychological analyses of the character of the spy (*The Secret Agent* [1907], *Under Western Eyes* [1911]), and themselves sometimes members of the Intelligence community yet politically liberal, writers such as Eric Ambler, Somerset Maugham, Geoffrey Household, and Graham Greene created portrayals of lonely, often cynical individuals who are hunted by both sides and who have lost much of their sprightly amateur status. In fact, some critics have pointed to this shift from amateur to professional status, from the writer's emphasis on "fair play" to a reliance on torture and violence, as indicating the demarcation between those writers who looked to *Tom Brown's Schooldays* for the classic pattern of plot and a later generation who were "willing to learn from the 'tough school' of American fiction, particularly from Hammett, Hemingway and Chandler."[2]

In Ken Follett's case, as we shall see, his deliberate cultivation of an American "tough guy" style in his earliest mysteries, as well as his later depiction of the professional spy as a lonely, even heartbroken individual (*The Man from St. Petersburg*), shows his indebtedness to this second group of writers, as do the recurrence of a hunter/hunted motif (even in works as recent as *The Third Twin* [1996] and *The Hammer of Eden* [1998]), and the liberal distrust of institutions.

A third generation of British espionage writers would include Ian Fleming, Len Deighton, and John Le Carré, whose post-World War II anxieties over empire, status, and class would be imposed on the genre in a number of ways: Fleming's latter-day Victorian, James Bond, would indulge in the unbridled consumerism, the technical gadgetry, and the sexual promiscuity of the post-war era while looking back nostalgically to the days of John Buchan and E. Phillips Oppenheim; Len Deighton would create an English hard-boiled hero with all of the fears and resentments of his American predecessors—an antagonism toward authority and a sense that romantic involvements are a trap; John Le Carré, like Joseph Conrad before him, would explore the many meanings of betrayal—sexual, political, and institutional, and would describe the continual aging of a pre-war academic who must live on in the present.

It is against this background of cynicism, even chauvinism, that Ken Follett inherited the espionage form, and while he has worked in other related genres, his principal contribution has been to the thriller. As we shall see, he has extended it through the inclusion of strong, believably drawn female characters; through the blending-in of love story elements and a general optimism towards romance; and through the expression of a post-1960s sexual egalitarianism that stands in marked contrast to either the schoolboy's adulation of the damsel-in-distress or the tough guy's disdain for "dames" and domesticity.

Popular literature has long reflected the attitudes and prejudices of its day, and the cultural change over a 25-year period can be traced in the changes in Follett's writing and publishing career. Today, writers such as Follett are taught in both high schools and colleges, and his political transformation, his current willingness to explicitly express a long-suppressed ideology in the context of his novels, reflects developments in mainstream British and American cultural life as well; in particular, the increasingly routine acceptance and application of literary theories which were considered leftist and radical a generation ago.

But this study is only nominally about ideology. It is instead about the growth, development and changes in a cultural figure not yet fifty who has been termed "a first-rate" writer of spy-thrillers and historical romances,[3] and one who, in his better work, "isn't ashamed to use all the traditional thriller devices of entertainment to serious ends—ideas about war, love, disappointment and hope."[4]

This tension between the popular and the serious underlies much of Follett's work and is part of the history of the genre: two traditions exist, not only conservative and liberal, but the traditions of the romance and the "realistic" work. A lineage can thus be sketched from the Puritan romance, *The Pilgrim's Progress,* to John Buchan to Ian Fleming and to Jeffrey Archer, where the emphasis is on the world as we would like it to be and on an allegorical journey that leads to the triumph of good over evil. A competing strain moves from Christopher Marlowe (and his deeply compromised Dr. Faustus) through Joseph Conrad, Graham Greene, and John Le Carré, writers who give us dramas about people who happen to be spies.

Follett has straddled these twin traditions, maintaining at times a perfect and at other times an uneasy balance, and an analysis of this conflict within the writing and within the individual's career remains central to this study.

By the 1970s, the spy novel had come to reflect an intense reader interest in covert operations aimed to topple foreign governments, and the "manhunt novel"—a story in which a secret agent on an impossible mission is tracked down, first established by H. C. McNeile and put to thematic purposes by Geoffrey Household and Graham Greene, was resurrected by Alister MacLean, Jack Higgins, and Frederick Forsyth, though often in the form of commandos on a suicide mission. Follett would find a plot and an inspiration in Forsyth's *The Day of the Jackal* (1971) and would be propelled at the age of twenty-nine to international bestseller status with the publication of *Eye of the Needle* (1978). But Follett, a dozen or more years younger than his closest competitors from the 1970s, would make two important changes in the covert operation story: unlike Higgins or Forsyth, whose British operatives struggle heroically against a foreign government and elude their pursuers, Follett would make the Nazi spy the hero for much of the tale and would suggest that the British government almost deserved to lose the war because of smugness and complacency. Second, he would introduce a strong female point-of-view to counter the essential "maleness" of these types of stories. Both innovations can be seen as the outcome of Follett's 1968 student protest experiences as well as the end product of years of serious literary experimentation, flexibility with form, and a willingness to attempt everything from science fiction to children's stories.

Follett was amazed to learn that the paperback rights to *Eye of the Needle* sold for more than Graham Greene's (paperback rights used to sell for), and he has quipped that there is no point in comparing himself to John Le Carré when he can compare himself to better writers.[5] Considered both a critical and popular success, *Eye of the Needle* was termed "quite simply the best spy novel to come out of England in years." Not only did it win the Edgar Allan Poe Award from the Mystery Writers of America, but the reprint edition alone sold 5.7 million copies. Although espionage novels from his middle period never quite fulfilled the artistic promise of his first international bestseller, he has been rated by John Cawelti and Bruce Rosenberg in their history of the form as one of the twenty best spy writers.[6] But the story of Follett's success is more than just the listing of numbers—his ranking compared to other writers, the number of copies sold, the number of dollars paid for three unwritten novels, etc.—it is the story of important artistic and personal transformations.

With the end of the Cold War in 1989, the espionage genre as it had been practiced for a generation had reached an impasse. A work such as James Park Sloan's *The Last Cold-War Cowboy* (1987) reflects, even in its title, an acute uncertainty regarding the longevity of the form. But Follett capably managed a transition to a post-Cold War mass-market readership. With the publication of *The Pillars of the Earth* in 1989, he moved more decidedly towards historical fiction, declaring that "[a]n historical novel is a much more difficult type of book to write than a thriller . . . , but it's also much more satisfying."[7] After a series of historical novels, Follett would bring those new writing experiences to the thriller form when he returned to it in 1996, reinvigorating the pattern through an even greater emphasis on a female consciousness and the inclusion of factual data more common to the historical novel.

Current popular forms can often be considered blends of earlier strains and the impact of other media on the Western, for example, and on the spy novel has been immense. Alfred Hitchcock mixed romantic comedy and the possibility of love into the film adaptation of Buchan's *The Thirty-Nine Steps* (1935); Michael Powell showed that the German spy in "The Spy in Black" (1939) could be so emotionally vulnerable as to jeopardize the outcome of an operation through an emotional entanglement. Follett, whose works have been termed "cinematic in conception,"[8] would not only expand upon such sources but would create his own unique hybrids. His mixing of the male-oriented thriller with the female-oriented category romance in *The Man from St. Petersburg,* his interest in applying contemporary thriller techniques to the historical novel in *A Dangerous Fortune* (1993) and *A Place Called Freedom* (1995), and his blending of the medical coverup story with the techno-thriller in *The Third Twin* (1996) are all examples of his versatility and experimentation. At times, this blending technique has allowed him to effectively resolve the struggle between melodrama and serious literature in ways reminiscent of the best examples of late 19th-century fiction.

Always quick to respond to market forces, the story of Follett's transmutation is also the story of changes in the publishing industry over a 25-year period; an industry that a generation ago still allowed for an independent publisher such as Arbor House to acquire the rights to a thriller by a then-unknown Welsh writer and promote it heavily; an industry that more recently has paid out enormous sums to writers such as Follett who now have celebrity status.

Follett has in part retained that status by changing the way he writes novels: initially attracted to both the terse style of the American hard-boiled novel as well as the more ornate "literariness" of a Joseph Conrad or a D. H. Lawrence, Follett has increasingly adapted himself to the expectations of an American mass-market audience. Follett once observed that his 1983 non-fiction book on a rescue operation organized by Ross Perot, *On Wings of Eagles,* changed the way he writes novels, especially the way he now uses dialogue,[9] and a careful reader will notice that the dialogue in *On Wings of Eagles* is almost entirely broad, slangy, clipped, and American. This kind of linguistic change that Follett refers to represents what has often taken place in popular writing, from Edgar Allan Poe to Brian Moore—the blurring of national literary distinctions. Interestingly, those film or television adaptations of Ken Follett's works which have been most successful have been those which have been most thoroughly "Americanized"—or perhaps, "internationalized" becomes the better term.

One final, yet equally important transformation needs to be anticipated here and discussed more specifically in subsequent pages: that change in Follett's political, ideological, and religious outlook as can help the reader interpret aspects of his work. An avowed atheist, Follett was raised in a strict, fundamentalist sect. A student protester at the University of London, Follett long suppressed his political leanings in a number of seemingly "conservative" espionage thrillers. Remarried in 1985 (to the widow of a slain South African activist), Follett has increasingly involved himself in contemporary British Labour Party politics. Not surprisingly, this newfound explicitness in expressing his views has at the very least added vitality and verve to his last few novels.

Such are the major divisions and themes of this book-length study, *Ken Follett: The Transformation of a Writer.* The structure of this book is roughly chronological, since Follett's career to date can be thought of as encompassing several phases: his apprenticeship novels up to *Eye of the Needle* (discussed in chapters 1 through 3), the paper-chase thrillers from *Eye of the Needle* through *Lie Down with Lions* (analyzed in chapters 4 through 8), and his "Robin Hood" thrillers, with their clearly egalitarian and leveling attitudes, from *The Pillars of the Earth* to the present (covered primarily in chapters 9, 10, and 11).

Two chapters in this book (5 and 6) are critiques of film or television adaptations of Follett's work, since dramatizations are themselves an interpretation and often tell us a great deal about the relative strengths and weaknesses of a source novel. In addition, Follett's relationship to film and other dramatic media is important not only for understanding his writing interests, but also for understanding his emergence as a popular cultural figure. These two chapters are thus included to demonstrate the convergence of literary and film criticism in popular culture studies and to provide a resource for those who are interested in related aspects of Follett's life and career.

The critical approach within each chapter of this book varies according to subject and theme. As a teacher of British Literature, Popular Culture, and Interpretive Writing, I have often cautioned my students to let the theory fit the text rather than the other way around. Certain texts beg for certain interpretations while the relentless and narrow application of rigid ideologies may result in, as we know, absurd symbol-hunting or the uncovering of non-existent conspiracies in largely innocuous material. In this study, I have attempted to follow my own advice: where a Freudian or Jungian approach seems appropriate, I have used it; so too, the Structuralist approach, the Feminist or Linguistic analysis, the Biographical approach, or the still-valid Formalist close reading.

These chapters were written at various times over the past decade, allowing me to observe the long-term development of Ken Follett's writing. Early drafts were first presented as conference papers or were published as journal articles but have since been extensively revised, expanded, and updated for this book-length study.

As such, I view these chapters as a series of reflections and observations on various aspects of Follett's work. Each chapter can be considered as self-contained, though the chapters taken together should add insight overall into the work of an important contemporary popular writer. In a number of instances, I have grouped his novels by topic: hence, a section on "The Art of the First Chapter," another on "Politics and Historical Revisionism," a third on stylistic and linguistic changes in his work overall and, as noted, chapters on film and television adaptations. Only a few of his novels are analyzed exclusively in chapters of their own: *The Big Needle* as his first novel, *Eye of the Needle* as perhaps his best, *The Man from St. Petersburg* because it is the clearest example of Follett's hybridization process, and *The Pillars of the Earth*, which stands alone in length, subject matter, and artistic strategy.

The challenge of writing on a living author is the same as when writing on any current and evolving situation, from political events to popular music: nations and rock bands dissolve, authors develop and reject favorite ideas. I have tried as much as possible to use direct quotations from Follett's numerous published interviews contemporaneously with the works under discussion in order to shed light on his thinking at a given time, though in some instances quotations from earlier or later periods offer interesting contrasts. This book is an analysis of representative works of Follett's fiction and of the films based on them, and the many other types of writing that have issued from his prolific pen—magazine articles, non-fiction books, television scripts—are discussed briefly and only as they help the reader better understand the development of his fiction.

1

INTRODUCTION AND OVERVIEW

Cardiff, with its National and Welsh Folk Museums and its famous castle, is both the repository of all-things-Welsh and the most ethnically blended location in Wales. Less than 15 miles from England across the Bristol Channel, Cardiff has long been populated by groups whose affinity with the Welsh language is non-existent—the Anglo-Saxons and their descendants, the Norman-French—and more recently, immigrants from the Indian subcontinent.

Although the Welsh language has been maintained in many families and in some chapels and schools, Kenneth Martin Follett was born on June 5, 1949, to an English-speaking household and was raised in a strict Evangelical sect with ties to southern England.[1] The surname "Follett" is Norman-French, though in other ways Ken Follett's linguistic, social, and educational background is representative of countless others in post-war Britain.

The son of a government tax inspector and a full-time homemaker, Follett has described his background as typically lower-middle class and as one characterized by the financial constraints of the time, though his grandfather, a wholesale grocer, made certain the family was never hungry. His sister, Hannah, who is four years younger, remembers Follett as a voracious reader who always did well in school, though Follett himself has said that he chafed against the rigidness of traditional schooling.[2] Regardless, as with many other talented working-class youths, he was able to advance through the British educational system then-in-place, with an aptitude test at the age of eleven, allowing for admission to a government-subsidized college-preparatory high school, followed by university (in Follett's case, the huge and prestigious state-supported University of London).

Essayist Richard Rodriguez, who completed his doctoral dissertation in Britain, has written at length on the experiences of "the scholarship boy"—that individual from a regional or working-class background who is blended-out of working-class life through the educational process. Citing the British educator Richard Hoggart, who studied such transitions in England in the 1950s, he describes the "neutralization" of accent and attitude that often occurs and the bi-polar world the scholarship boy is forced to inhabit.[3] For some individuals, such as Rodriguez, such a division has proven troubling; other individuals may have learned to move more comfortably between cultures and worlds.

Certainly, in Ken Follett's mature writing, there is little to suggest a strong regional or class identification: a central character in *The Pillars of the Earth* is Welsh, but there are several other equally important English characters in that lengthy novel; a sympathy for the poor and the downtrodden manifests itself in the novels following the financial success of *The Pillars of the Earth,* but those characters are Cockney, Jewish, Scottish, and American. Unlike a writer such as Dylan Thomas, who even in his prose attempts to capture the flamboyance and the rhythms of Welsh-accented speech, or the Welsh-born critic Raymond Williams, whose essays are almost entirely about class, the bulk of Follett's work is comparatively neutral linguistically and ideologically.

What does strike one, however, in listening to Follett's voice is his extreme flexibility with accent. Explaining the origins of his first novel, *The Big Needle,* to a live British audience, Follett's speech takes on the intonations and inflections of Received Pronunciation (R.P.), a learned accentuation devoid of either regional or class markers: "I hope none of you *ever* get to read *that* novel!" When promoting his novels on American television, Follett's speech is peppered with Americanisms ("You bet!") and American stress patterns: "The old stuff was *terr*ible!" and the accent itself can perhaps best be described as tight, nonregional and transatlantic.[4]

Though Rodriguez is critical of the scholarship boy's erasure of authentic accent, terming that person "a bad student . . . a mimic; a collector of thoughts, not a thinker,"[5] such multi-dialectalism can be a strength for a novelist. Today, Follett divides his time between his home in London and a second residence in New York.

As I have suggested, Follett's career can be thought of as encompassing several stages: a period of apprenticeship, experimentation, and rapid development culminating in the publication of an international bestseller; a middle period of some self-imitation and generic patterning, prompting a number of reviewers to term those works disappointing, inferior, or simply unworthy of his talent;[6] and a period of new directions.

Follett's performance has been called "somewhat uneven,"[7] and a central consideration in assessing a popular writer, in addition to speculating on the various reasons for mass appeal, would be to determine the quality of the product. One measure of literary value is, of course, the use of language, where "aesthetic" and "efficient" would be equally valued terms so long as the style is matched to purpose.

In the following pages of this introductory chapter, we will engage in a linguistic and stylistic analysis of representative passages from Follett's novels in order to suggest some of the peaks and valleys in his career and to trace his overall development as a writer. Relevant and probable influences on his writing style will also be discussed.

An obvious influence, for example, is that of education and training, which, taken together, might suggest a tension in his work and writing style. When Follett graduated from the University of London in 1970 with an honors degree in Philosophy, he began work as a trainee journalist at the *South Wales Echo*. As a student, Follett had read Henry James and Virginia Woolf, as well as popular novelists, but now needed to learn "newspaper fluency."[8] Culture critic Leo Lowenthal, in his classic work *Literature, Popular Culture, and Society* (1961), has discussed the conflict between an academic writing style and the demands of journalism, observing that increasingly in the 20th century the "language of promotion has replaced the language of evaluation." Follett himself has concurred that journalism is both the best and the worst training ground for an aspiring fiction writer. He returned to London in 1973 to work as a crime reporter for the now defunct tabloid, the *Evening News,* and developed a flowing, fast-paced newspaper style which he later termed "too facile in a novel."[9]

Already married at age eighteen, and by 1973 the father of two children, Follett felt compelled to look for other sources of income. Encouraged by the success of a fellow reporter who had sold a mystery novel, within weeks Follett wrote and sold *The Big Needle* under the pseudonym "Symon Myles." This crime story about a heroin dealer is analyzed in detail in chapter 2, and while there are passages in *The Big Needle* of a more elevated, literary prose, the novel for the most part predictably is written in the fast-paced, breezy newspaper style which Follett says he later had to "unlearn,"[10] as the following section makes clear:

Crown Terrace is an old street in the East End. Most of the property has been turned into small factories and beat-up offices or left empty to rot. Number 17 I had bought in a package, and I hadn't been able to do anything with it.[11]

In addition to the short sentences, what makes this passage read like newspaper-writing is, of course, the use of the simple present tense and summary narration rather than description. "Newspaper writing," Follett has reflected, "requires the bare facts stated concisely. In writing novels, I [later] had to learn to linger at climactic scenes."[12] Even here, however, the use of a first person narrator, a technique drawn largely from American hard-boiled detective fiction, shifts this passage from simple reporting to storytelling.

Using the same pseudonym, Follett wrote two other novels in *The Big* series (*The Big Black* [1974] and *The Big Hit* [1975]). He then left journalism for a young publishing company, Everest Books, where "nobody knew anything about publishing because we were all out of journalism." But "the language of promotion" stood him in good stead: "[W]e knew how to promote, we knew the media, and that saved us."[13]

Over the next five years, Follett worked at Everest Books as an editor and continued to develop his own prose style, moving gradually back toward "the language of evaluation" and what he has called the need in popular fiction for "grace, insight and conviction." Not all of his early works achieve those ends. His two children's books, *The Power Twins* and *The Secret of Kellerman's Studio* (both published in 1976), are understandably devoid of literary embellishment. A science fiction novel, *Capricorn One* (1978), written under the pseudonym "Bernard L. Ross" and actually a "novelization" of an existing screenplay, is workman-like and undistinguished, though one might argue that "conviction" is present in the scathing denunciation of the city of Houston as a "whore" wearing "cheap scent" and throwing "lavish" but "tedious" parties.[14] Most of it, however, remains journalistic.

Even in his tenth novel, *The Modigliani Scandal,* published in 1976 under the nom de plume "Zachary Stone," there is "a tendency to underwrite," which Follett has suggested has characterized many of his apprenticeship novels. In a brief review of *The Modigliani Scandal* mystery writer H. R. F. Keating noted, however, that the novel contained that "essential read-on quality" despite its emphasis on explanation.[15]

This is a fairly typical expository passage from *The Modigliani Scandal:*

The rubber came away from the bottom of the stamp. Peter found a large envelope on a shelf. He put the notepaper and the thin slice of rubber into the envelope and sealed it. He took a pen from another box and wrote Mitch's name and address on the envelope. Then he closed the steel cupboard door, picked up his ream of forms, and went out.[16]

Obviously, much of this still depends on summary narration and on the compactness noticeable in journalism. Looking at the paragraph more scrupulously, we can observe that this unadorned style is the result of two simple sentences of ten words and eight words which begin the passage, and then are followed by three sentences of sixteen words each. Those three subsequent sentences, however, each have the feel of much shorter sentences since all three remain compound sentences reliant on the coordinating conjunction "and." The slight variety in the last sentence is achieved by avoiding "and" once in the compound predicate.

Another measure of the relative sparseness of the writing style is the ratio between narrative prose and dialogue. In *The Modigliani Scandal,* there is a great deal more dialogue—roughly three quarters of the page on average—than there is exposition.

Paper Money, written the following year (1977) and about an ambitious young reporter for a London newspaper, is stylistically still reliant on simple sentences, resulting in what one reviewer termed "a quick and entertaining read."[17] But these simple sentences are now balanced out by many more concrete nouns, complex sentences, and subordinate clauses, as in this example:

With a warehouse full of expensive electronic gadgetry for which he had paid nothing, he held a sale. Record players, color television sets, digital clocks, tape decks, amplifiers, and radios went for knockdown prices, sometimes as little as half their retail value. In two days the warehouse was empty and Tony Cox had three thousand pounds in cash in two suitcases. He locked the warehouse and went home.[18]

During this same period of time, Follett was not only writing capers, children's stories, and science fiction books under pseudonyms and at the rate of two books per year, he was starting to feel sufficiently confident in his craft to issue novels under his own name. *The Shakeout* (1975) and *The Bear Raid* (1976), two novels about industrial espionage that appear to be strongly influenced by the serious literary concerns of British social realism (see chapter 3), contain numerous descriptive passages that seem primarily aesthetic or atmospheric in purpose. In addition, narrative prose seems at the very least the equal of dialogue, and passages of conversation are often integrated with description and reflection, giving a certain fullness to the text.

Even in *Paper Money,* a novel which Follett has said was "painted in brisk, bold brushstrokes,"[19] there is now as much narrative prose as dialogue, and in some chapters narrative prose predominates and dialogue is kept to a minimum.

Follett had learned to "linger" at important scenes and to incorporate a number of stylistic techniques—description, narration, reflection as well as to use dialogue. Notice the advancement in technique in a passage from *Eye of the Needle,* published the following year (1978):

The bridesmaids had something of that look, too; they were country girls. But the bride was like her mother. Her hair was dark, dark red, long and thick and shining and glorious, and she had wide-apart amber eyes and an oval face; and when she looked at the vicar with that clear, direct gaze and said, "I will" in that firm, clear voice, the vicar was startled and thought "By God she means it!" which was an odd thought for a vicar to have in the middle of the wedding.[20]

The passage becomes absolutely literary, not just because we begin with a compound sentence, then find it balanced by a simple sentence and a long complex sentence that forms the bulk of the paragraph, nor because of the artful repetition "dark, dark hair" and the precise description "amber eyes," but because we have something else as well: a masterful control of point-of-view, shifting from Lucy's perspective to the vicar's, that allows the author to create irony through authorial detachment: it was "an odd thought for a vicar to have in the middle of the wedding." The book, on balance, maintains this "literariness" without an overreliance on dialogue for its own sake.

For several years, this work represented Follett's artistic high point, with its skillful balance of the popular and the serious, the literary and the fast-paced. Although the success of the novel must to a certain extent be attributed to a deft promotional campaign as well as to a heightened American public interest in world events during the OPEC oil crisis and the taking of U.S. hostages in Iran, the critical success of *Eye of the Needle* is no doubt due in part to its "occasionally felicitous prose."[21]

Apparently eager to capitalize on his first international success, Follett reworked the formula and its wartime settings in a number of thrillers written during the late 1970s and early 1980s, ones which were often placed in the Middle East or in the Islamic world. Some reviewers noticed a staleness and a "coarsening of his no-frills prose." Having written three thrillers in quick succession (*Triple* [1979], *The Key to Rebecca* [1980], and *The Man from St. Petersburg* [1982]), Follett has said he "was tired of it and [was] looking for something different" when he was fortuitously presented with the opportunity to research and write *On Wings of Eagles,* an extensive project which he considered a break from novels. In the preface to the book, Follett noted that his work of nonfiction records "what really happened," but that real-life conversation needs to be reconstructed and edited. The two-year immersion in the diction of American "businessmen—slightly macho, who are not quick to tell you about their emotional lives . . . ," and what a reviewer called "the painstaking job of reporting,"[22] seemingly influenced his writing style when he returned to novels in 1985.

Lie Down with Lions is a case in point. The prose narration in that novel almost represents a return to his early reporter's style, as in this passage:

He glanced at the clock. He was early. In his mind he ran over his plan. If all went well, today would be the triumphant conclusion to more than a year of patient, careful work. And he would be able to share that triumph with Jane, if he was still alive at the end of the day.[23]

Moreover, the selection of an American character for the novel allows the writer to continue to work in that taciturn and idiomatic speaking style that he had recorded in *On Wings of Eagles*. "[He remembered] why he was so tense" (6) and "[She couldn't get] any kind of commitment from him" (11) are rather typical examples of the way the prose is Americanized, or rather, "conversationalized." During this period of time, Follett's books consistently sold much better in the United States than in Britain, and on several occasions he expressed a keen interest in extending and pleasing his readership. On the other hand, as his agent and long-time friend, Al Zuckerman, has put it, Follett "has ambition— to write better books and to sell more copies. . . . He likes to move on and he is enormously hard-working." By 1985, the same year he divorced his first wife and married Barbara Broer, the widow of a murdered South African civil rights leader, he alluded in a *New York Times* book review to "the pleasures and many of the irritations we expect from the [thriller] genre." In fact, he has indicated that by the time he finished *Lie Down with Lions* he felt he had nothing new to say in the spy-thriller format.[24]

Clearly, it was time for a change since "writing tales of derring-do is a constant struggle against implausibility, not to say absurdity," as he put it. Wales has more castles in a small area than any other part of Britain and perhaps that accounts for Follett's early interest in medieval architecture, going back to the 1970s, if not before. Throughout the period of his paper-chase novels, Follett was toying with the idea of writing a novel about the building of a medieval cathedral and read "'several hundred books' on the Middle Ages, particularly on church architecture,"[25] an intensive reading which would have had an impact on his writing style as he composed *The Pillars of the Earth,* a 400,000-word historical romance set in 12th-century England.

The density of the writing is in part the result of thorough detailing and of full, descriptive paragraphs. While the style itself has to be assessed as "contemporary," there are occasional touches of syntactic sophistication which move it beyond ordinary newspaper prose, as in the elegant periodic sentence which begins chapter 1: "In a broad valley, at the foot of a sloping hillside, beside a clear bubbling stream, Tom was building a house."[26]

Follett's reading today is a mixture of contemporary and 19th-century literature: he lists American writers such as Larry McMurty and Pat Conroy, as well as the Brazilian Jorge Amado as favorites, but also looks to the Victorian novelists George Eliot, Jane Austen, and Charles Dickens, whom he reads while writing "in a vain attempt to be influenced."[27] Perhaps Follett's novels since 1985 can best be assessed as a blend of British and American styles, alternately historical or contemporary in setting.

Sometimes, this blending of dialects and his desire to meet readership needs in the United States has resulted in some anachronisms of phraseology. *Night Over Water,* published in 1991, is a difficult book to categorize, stylistically or otherwise. Coming after the fullness of *The Pillars of the Earth,* it seems a temporary retreat, or interlude. According to Follett, *Night Over Water* is not even a thriller per se, but rather "a moving vehicle story" like *Ship of Fools* or *Murder on the Orient Express.* Set in 1939 on a transatlantic flight originating in Britain, the novel nevertheless contains such recent American diction as "[she didn't want to] marry some pig who thought he had the right to boss her around" and "she longed for a different kind of relationship."[28] In addition, and perhaps as a kind of updating technique, comma splices are frequently used within conversation. Most sentences begin "he" or "she" and follow a standard subject, verb, object pattern. Past tense is created through simple helping verbs, as in "had taken" or "had had." The whole emphasis, therefore, seems to be on readability—on speed—and a typical paragraph describing action is comprised of only three simple sentences, none of them much longer than a dozen words: "He stepped onto the platform. The rope was tied to a capstan sticking up from the nose of the aircraft. He untied it rapidly" (388).

In that novel, at least, Follett appeared to have returned to the stylistic approach which had served him well on newspapers. More sure-footed, both in terms of the use of American diction and narrative prose, is his 1996 thriller *The Third Twin,* set largely in Baltimore. Although the occasional British idiom still lingers— "jumper"[29] for "sweater" or "you had to look smart" (11) for "look sharp," the product appears to have been as thoroughly Americanized as possible, from the inclusion of contemporary campus and feminist attitudes toward the power structure, to word-choice that seems almost self-consciously current and youth-oriented: "What a downer . . ." (348), "Oh, gross" (292), and "Am I a weirdo?" (68). In the acknowledgements page of the book, Follett lists among his many readers and editors his "oldest collaborator and sharpest critic" (469), the American agent Al Zuckerman as well as his children and step-children, one of whom, Jann Turner, presently lives in the United States. The many other readers whom he thanks are almost all American and no doubt aided in a linguistic "fine-tuning."

The language of the two historical novels set primarily in Britain, *A Dangerous Fortune* (1993) and *A Place Called Freedom* (1995), reverses this process, as one might expect from a writer who recognizes the subtleties of tone and style. The "English" quality of the language in *A Dangerous Fortune* is most apparent in the dialogue, which uses the deliberate markers of British "Received Pronunciation"—precise word choice, appositives or absolute phrases, and a tone of authority—to demonstrate the character's identification with power, education, and material success: "'He was a lovely boy—comely, kind, high-born and rich. Naturally his parents were horrified at the prospect that he should marry a grocer's daughter.'"[30]

In these historical novels, this "Britishness" surfaces in expository sections as well, as an example from *A Place Called Freedom* makes clear:

Sitting on a three-legged stool, smelling of sandalwood and swinging a shapely leg, was Peg's red-haired friend Cora, in a chestnut-colored coat and a jaunty hat. . . . Because of her striking coloring and her dashing clothes, she attracted a lot of attention, and Mack got envious looks from other men.[31]

The balanced sentence which begins the above selection stands in obvious contrast to the "lean and driven" prose[32] of more Americanized works such as *Night Over Water*. The word choice "jaunty," "coloring," and "dashing" also suggests an interest in using more British forms. These last few historical novels have also enjoyed improved sales in Britain.[33]

Follett has sometimes also blended a more elevated literary style for authorial commentary with a more colloquial Americanized style for character dialogue or thought. In *The Hammer of Eden* (1998), the expository statement "He was not suspicious, then; but he was apprehensive, and . . . marked his frustration with a show of nonchalance" is set side-by-side with the casual sentence "You going to the bar tonight?"[34] —a juxtaposition which Follett puts to considerable effect.

But whether writing in contemporary American diction or suggesting the tones and structure of the language as used in the British Isles, the question of his treatment of sex in his novels has continued to dog him, a controversy which can also be addressed through an analysis of style. Novelist John Braine has offered the familiar advice to aspiring writers that human sexuality needs to be treated with a fair degree of tact in fiction since what matters most is the thoughts of the characters rather than the actual physical positions. When asked if his novels contain a fixed number of sex scenes according to some formula, Follett has answered that he writes "explicit love scenes because sex reveals character," but throughout his career he has been accused of marring otherwise fine works by the inclusion of gratuitous, sensationalistic, and sometimes even fetishistic sex.[35]

In terms of literary treatment, the lovemaking scenes in his novels which most "reveal character" and character change would seem to be the ones which are internalized, subdued, and evocative, as in *Eye of the Needle,* rather than those descriptions which tend to focus almost exclusively on external details and on physical surroundings, as in *Night Over Water*. Regardless, the depiction of sex in his novels varies somewhat from work to work, thus demonstrating an interest in perfecting his craft.

Such variation throughout his career indicates that the topography of his writing has changed over the years, and will probably continue to do so. This seems natural given his early experimentation and mixing of genres, his flexibility with language and his willingness to attempt new forms. "I may do something completely different," he predicted in 1983. "I would like to be writing for the next 40 years, and I certainly do not intend to follow any kind of formula for that period of time. . . . I'm constrained by what I think are the preferences of my readers [but] if I'm careful, I'll take them along with me."[36]

2

WRITING AS "SYMON MYLES":
WHAT ENGLAND BORROWED AND RETURNED

The evolution of Follett's craft can best be understood through an analysis of his earliest published work and through a discussion of those cultural and literary influences that probably helped form it.

Dissatisfied personally and professionally by the low standards of the newspaper he was working for,[1] and pressured financially when his car broke down, Follett knew that "one of my fellow reporters had written a thriller on the side and sold it, so I decided to try my hand."[2] The result of his efforts was a mystery-thriller called *The Big Needle* (1974), which he sold for £200.

As one might expect, this first novel is more imitative than original, and is deeply grounded in the cultural and popular literary currents of the day.

Follett has stated that the greatest event of his lifetime was the Vietnam war, which radicalized him, but that as with many young people starting out, during the 1970s he was focused primarily on his career.[3] Nevertheless, the loosening-up of social constraints during the late 1960s and early 1970s was extensive in Britain. The impact of television, the increased acceptance of drug use, the rise of political protest groups, as well as the evolution of international youth culture through popular music, fashion, and film have all been cited as important cultural factors in the England of Follett's formative years. Dennis Kavanagh, for example, in his text "Political Culture in Great Britain" (1980), has concluded that throughout the period "the old restraints of hierarchy and deference" were "waning."[4]

Changes in literary tastes, and the ensuing relaxation of fixed writing standards, would have also been equally extensive. Those harbingers of "the American Age," which Jimmy Porter complains of in the play *Look Back in Anger* (1956), must include writers such as Dashiell Hammett, Raymond Chandler, and Mickey Spillane, all of whom helped popularize the American "hard-boiled" style and who had a large international following, with Mickey Spillane's total sales, for example, amounting to more than 150 million novels sold worldwide.[5] As a result, the impact on the British thriller was considerable: Ian Fleming's James Bond has been compared to Spillane's Mike Hammer in terms of the love of guns, the parade of loyal secretaries and compliant females, and the ritualized, cathartic violence; Len Deighton's Bernard Samson shares the emotional detachment, the sarcasm, and the resentment of the rich with Chandler's Phillip Marlowe. Even the early works of John Le Carré, with their emphasis on solving a crime and on the agent Alec Leamas as a man of toughness, action and fundamental world-weariness, show a connection with American hard-boiled writers.

Follett, who has said that he "was a great liver in fantasy worlds from an early age," was well acquainted with popular novels: he began reading H. G. Wells' stories at the age of seven, and by the time he was eleven was especially fond of the American-influenced Ian Fleming.[6] Throughout the 1950s and 1960s, the years of Follett's schooling, cultural contact with American popular forms had been intensified in Britain through television, radio, film, and above all advertising so that, as one advertiser put it, the "depiction of American life, or at least the popular myth of American life . . . all looked very attractive and . . . was associated with American products."[7] In terms of popular literature and the dissemination of their patterns and styles, such superselling authors of the late 1960s and early 1970s as Mario Puzo, Peter Benchley, Erich Segal and Jacqueline Susann had all been marketed internationally as if they were a product line, resulting in some change in reading tastes in other countries. Follett has indicated that even during his university days, he longed to set aside more traditional reading for such sensational mysteries as Mickey Spillane's *My Gun Is Quick*.[8]

Looking back to his literary origins, Follett has argued "that there is no one formula or method" for success, but that he did learn to write good books "by writing mediocre ones and wondering what was wrong with them." According to his agent, Al Zuckerman, for the five years that Follett worked as an editor at Everest Books, he produced, on average, two "sub-Mickey Spillane" paperback originals a year which remained primarily minor successes restricted to an English readership.[9] The surface similarities between such early works as *The Big Needle* and the super-selling novels of Mickey Spillane are clear even when considering storyline:

The hero of *The Big Needle,* Chadwell Carstairs, learns that his daughter, Jane, is near death because of having overdosed on heroin. Swearing revenge, Carstairs—a building contractor and real estate investor who lives a hip counterculture lifestyle—follows the drug trail from local supplier to international source in Marseilles, then back to

London. Having bought up and smuggled in vast quantities of heroin in order to create a crisis in the market, Carstairs discovers that the man closest to him, Detective Inspector Lambourne, is the real Mr. H. After a car chase, Carstairs kills Lambourne and is reconciled with his estranged daughter, who has recovered from the overdose.

This plot summary alone suggests three key parallels with Mickey Spillane's novels. John G. Cawelti, in his seminal work *Adventure, Mystery and Romance* (1976), described the Spillane formula as: a) the hero pursues an investigation that leads him ever deeper into the perversion and evil endemic to the urban setting; b) the search is initiated by sentimental feelings, such as deep sorrow for a murdered friend, and; c) the hero's search is outside the law and involves brutality and cathartic violence.[10] A closer examination of Follett's text will reveal that *The Big Needle* shares other characteristics with Mickey Spillane's novels, such as a lower-class suspicion of urban elites and minority groups, as well as a preoccupation with sex, violence, and social status.

Follett begins *The Big Needle,* and his career as a novelist, with the words: "The air in the bedroom was cold when I poked my nose over the edge of the quilt. I wondered whether the central heating had gone on the blink" (5). We find in these two sentences two of the most familiar conventions of the hard-boiled detective genre: number one, what Kenneth Van Dover calls the use of the "imperative first person" to create a reductive "solipsistic universe" through which all perceptions and events are filtered (95); and number two, a shabby genteel atmosphere that Cawelti suggests "may look like failure, but . . . is actually rebellion, a rejection of the ordinary concepts of success and respectability" (144).

The use of first person narration is especially significant given Follett's subsequent avoidance of it in almost all his later work. If our initial assumption as readers that we are in the familiar world of shabby offices on the margin of a city's business district later proves to be a false one, the clue is there nonetheless. Follett has often expressed embarrassment about the structural inconsistencies in his early writing:

I remember in one book I started off making the heroine have green eyes, then, forty pages on, I forgot and gave her brown eyes. Instead of going back to correct it, I wrote a line further on in the book where the hero looks at her and says "You have brown eyes, but I thought you had green eyes." Of course I wouldn't think of doing that now. My publisher wouldn't allow it.[11]

As we shall see, some of the inconsistencies in *The Big Needle* are stylistic as well as structural and suggest an early ambiguity concerning genre, literary models, and cultural attitudes.

Initially, the writing style in *The Big Needle* seems self-consciously Spillane-esque. The numerous borrowed Americanisms are no doubt intended to suggest a cynical tough-guy banter, such as "Jane OD-ed on horse" (10) or "So you haven't become AC/DC yet?" (38) but occasionally result in awkward transmutations such as "He's as queer as a five-bob note" (37). Where the writing style seems especially formulaic is in the descriptions of the periodic violence—the sadism, in fact—that is a hallmark of the Spillane product-line, as in this passage: "I took a quick step forward and swung at him with the spanner. It smashed into his mouth, breaking a couple of teeth. He yelped with pain and put his hands to his bleeding face" (117). We find here the same "taut vernacular . . . , short, staccato sentences, rhythmic repetitions, and rapid pace" (Cawelti 175) considered a central characteristic of the tough-guy detective style. In passages that introduce the formulaic element of moral indignation and revenge as motivation, the word choice and sentence structure become pure formula as well. Follett writes: "I would find that bastard. And I would kill him" (13).

But imitation pure and simple would probably have resulted only in parody and in a counterfeit American product that might well have been rejected by a British reading public. Instead, in *The Big Needle,* there are a number of emendations to the formula, a number of blendings, that have "nativized" it to create domestic, or at least generational, appeal.

Britain, during the ten-year time-frame from about 1966 to 1976, was a society undergoing considerable cultural change. Not only was there concern over relative economic decline, but there was also the radicalizing of a whole generation of young Britons who came into conflict with the police at political rallies. The development of a viable counterculture and the hardening of anti-establishment attitudes is well-known. Two examples from popular British films from the period, "Blow-Up" (1966) and "Performance" (1968), suggest attitudes and images common to the era and which find their way into *The Big Needle.*

For example, moments after encountering the archetypal hard-boiled detective setting, the cold water flat, the reader finds out that the room is decorated with "trendy, plastic and horribly uncomfortable chair[s]" (7)—the type of pop-art furniture frequently made visible in "Blow-Up" or in other films from the era. More importantly, the hero of the novel, Carstairs, like the David Hemmings character in "Blow-Up" as well as "Mr. Turner" (played by Mick Jagger) in "Performance," represents the loosening of traditional sexual constraints. All three characters, at one point or another, are participants in tripartite sex. The image of the three-way liaison seems prevalent in the popular culture of the time and stands in direct opposition to conventional marital pairings. In addition, the unencumbered sexual encounter is often used to suggest the blurring of conservative borders, whether social, racial, or sexual.

In "Blow-Up," for example, the photographer moves from partner to partner and across the various levels of society. Carstairs' two partners also come from divergent ends of the social scale; one is "a true aristocrat" (5) and the other a Jamaican black. Racially, the Britain depicted in any of these three examples from popular culture is clearly the "post-immigration" Britain of the 1960s and 1970s: the rock musician in "Performance" is black; the nightclub scene in "Blow-Up" highlights interracial couples dancing; and Carstairs, in *The Big Needle,* listens to "Bab's Jamaican accent" (10) and visits a doctor who "was a tall, tired Asian with a bald head" (12).

In all three works, not only is there an indication of bi-sexuality to show a further breaking down of traditional boundaries, but also the sexual engagements tend to take place in unconventional surroundings: the photographer's set in "Blow-Up" and the bathtub in both "Performance" and *The Big Needle,* where it is described as "big enough for three—by design" (19).

Such images complicate and undercut the Spillane form, and references to popular taste in fashion and music show additional ways in which the genre is being blended. The type of outlandish dress—the varicolored vinyl and rainbow striped pants—shown in "Blow-Up" or "Performance" is worn proudly by Carstairs who dons, at various times, "navy flared trousers" (22), "a T-shirt [with] some fancy jewellry" (23), and "a jacket with enormous white buttons" (151). As with other members of the counterculture, Carstairs uses fashion to make a nonconformist statement: one of his T-shirts has a hammer and sickle on the front (25). If the desire to write both a crime story and an underground novel results in confusing signals, Follett at least understood the division within the culture and was able to project those confusions onto character: Carstairs' business partner, we are told, had "a split personality. He didn't know whether to be a staid, responsible business type like accountants are supposed to be; or to be a trendy young professional, as befitted someone who had risen as far and as fast as he had" (55).

The division between the old and the new applies to Carstairs himself. Like the photographer in "Blow-Up," who moves between antique shops and abstract art studios, or the aging rock star in "Performance," who buys paintings but composes *avant-garde* songs, Carstairs is both a collector of the old (113) and an afficionado of the new. If the fundamental dichotomy between age and youth is visually emphasized in "Blow-Up," where no actors appear to be over thirty except the establishment figure (a businessman or possibly a politician) who significantly enough is slain in the park, this generational split, as evidenced by fashion, is also present in *The Big Needle*. Carstairs sports "a Zapata moustache" that is grey (16) and when standing next to a suntanned youth who is twenty years his junior becomes suddenly aware of his "pot belly and scraggy legs" (7).

"Newness," the sixties' fascination with novelty for its own sake, is most apparent in the references to music in these examples from British popular culture. "The Yardbirds" and Jagger's songs are a prominent part of the atmosphere in "Blow-Up" and "Performance" respectively, and in *The Big Needle*, David Bowie (37), Eric Clapton (99), "The Who" (87), "Cream" (58) and "The Beatles" (40) are cited specifically and become part of the cultural milieu.

Rapid cultural change can result in an individual's anger or confusion—or at the very least, uncertainty—and characters in these three narrative examples attempt to negotiate different worlds, with varying degrees of success. The gangster in "Performance" is the least adept at moving between the "square world" and the "hip world" and is destroyed as a result. The photographer in "Blow-Up," who is shown in the guise of an unemployed factory worker, then as a member of the art scene, initially appears to be comfortable in all spheres, but the film moves increasingly into ambiguity. In *The Big Needle* a character is described as "trying to belong to two worlds: the world of the embassies and the world of [designers and pushers] . . . Before long one of the two worlds would reject him" (78).

In essence, the societal fragmentation of the 1960s results in a moral ambivalence toward drugs, sex, and even wealth in *The Big Needle* and in a dilution of the standard Spillane formula. For example, what Van Dover calls the "self-righteous rapture of [the] Old Testament scourge" (127) expressed by a Mike Hammer is here compromised by Carstairs' own drug use and the attitude that "a couple of blasts wouldn't hurt" (43). What Cawelti terms the "righteous chastity" (185) underlying a Spillane thriller is, in *The Big Needle*, diminished by Carstairs' sexual liberality and desire to "corrupt" Babs (61). The unrelenting drive toward the resolution of the mystery in a hard-boiled detective novel is, in "Blow-Up," "Performance," or *The Big Needle*, often put on hold because of the need to show the personal exploration and sexual experimentation associated with the sixties. In other words, if a Spillane novel is metaphorically "a striptease," as Cawelti puts it, where sexual provocation can be fulfilled only in violence (184-85), the central image for this early Follett thriller is the group sexual encounter, which frequently distracts the hero from his violent quest.

This pleasure-seeking results in some odd contrasts within the book so that when Carstairs stops to spend the night with a young hitchhiker, described as "young and innocent and continually bubbling over" (90), there is no thought of Carstairs' dying daughter, who had been described in much the same way. And when Carstairs does reflect on his daughter "falling into an early grave on the point of the big needle" (155), the image and the subtext are inconsistent with his stated need in the very next paragraph for a stiff drink and "an *injection* of savagery" (155 [emphasis added]). Clearly, the primary plot-line drawn from Spillane requires that hedonism be portrayed negatively; the cultural influences from the 1960s argue for a greater permissiveness—and the competing strains within the novel tend to cancel each other out.

Deeply imbedded contradictions result from the inclusion of another formulaic ingredient: Spillane's "nativist hatred of racial and ethnic minorities" (Cawelti 190) and from his prejudice against homosexuals. The recipient of the violence cited earlier is, as per the recipe, "a negro . . . [who] wore a dinner jacket and a black bow tie" (116), but what might in other cases be an example of "the casual racism endemic in the tough-guy fiction of the thirties and forties" (Van Dover 104) is, in *The Big Needle,* negated by the presence of British "New Left" attitudes, which developed during the 1960s.

The issues for the New Left were primarily international rather than exclusively domestic, and included nuclear proliferation, racism in South Africa, and American involvement in Vietnam. For many New Left thinkers, increased tolerance toward racial and sexual minorities was also an important tenet.

Follett has indicated that he was a passive socialist during this period of time,[12] but he actively expresses liberal attitudes toward race and sexuality in this first novel, transforming it from a pure Spillane derivation.

When Carstairs, for example, hears a racial epithet used toward an African head-of-state, he decides that he doesn't have "the patience to argue with bigots" (22). Later, he comes across a T-shirt he had given Babs that reads "'End race hate—miscegenate'" (114), and is driven to violence because of her abduction.

Although the bigotry required by the formula results in Carstairs' catching hold of "this little poof [and swinging] him around against the wall" (118), in non-generic fashion Carstairs' has also kissed "the biggest queer in London" (125) on the mouth because "it gave him a thrill and cost me nothing" (37). This open acknowledgement of sexual duality in the hero seems a far remove from the seething sexual repression of a Mike Hammer who, in the notorious trick ending to *Vengeance*

Is Mine (1950), shoots "the best looking thing I ever saw"[13] when it turns out that "*Juno was a man!*" (176).

But if these two aspects of the American formula—sexual tension and cathartic violence—seem muddled through transplantation to the hip London scene, class antagonisms are, if anything, intensified.

Some social critics have argued that changes in Britain during the 1960s were largely superficial, involving a coating of American popular culture for the young, but that "the political culture remain[ed] predominantly an allegiant one,"[14] with the traditional sharp distinctions of social class still intact. However, with some increased opportunities for advancement, the concern with social mobility and strata perhaps became even more obsessive in the post-war period than at other times, as evidenced by the numerous popular novels, plays, and films which specifically address this issue: *Room at the Top* (1957), *A Taste of Honey* (1958), "Saturday Night and Sunday Morning" (1958), *This Sporting Life* (1960), *Chips with Everything* (1962), "Alfie" (1965), and so forth.

Though Britain is probably no more class-ridden than many other Western European countries (Germany, France, and Spain come to mind), the *consciousness* of class may indeed be more heightened, with people quick to label one another through a number of signs, such as clothing, education, interests, type of car, manners—and above all, accent.

Carstairs, therefore, and despite a more egalitarian counterculture outlook, is still able to sniff out "an undertone of Cockney" beneath a refined accent (69) and a genuine "Home Countries [sic]" intonation worthy of a "middle-ranking civil servant" (158). His awareness of speech as related to status is keen, and he tells us that "my Cockney accent" is faked while "my BBC English" is "for real," explaining that he "was born into a classy family which went bankrupt" (34). There is a great deal of wish-fulfillment in the novel, the "fantasy world" that Follett once referred to: the use of the terms "classy" and "for real" are themselves probably an indication of lower socio-economic speech, and Carstairs seems genuinely relieved once in Wales when he can change out of his display of upper middle-class success and into the authentic dress of a workman—"heavy denim jeans"—and can comment enthusiastically on it in relaxed regional speech—"*yer* actual slimline Wranglers, none of this fancy flared rubbish" (138 [emphasis added]).

Mystery writers from Edgar Allan Poe to Ian Fleming and John Le Carré have created heroes who were superior to themselves in education or in social standing, and the projection of anxieties is a common psychological as well as literary phenomenon. At a time when the young Ken Follett was without the money to retrieve his own car from a repair shop, he creates the persona of a "rich, middle-aged trendy" (21) who gets a "kick from hearing [his] Jaguar's 12 cylinders hum effortlessly into life" (11) and who later drives a Ferrari (151). Although this name brand snobbery is in part a formulaic ingredient from the James Bond series, as are the references to "an incredibly good meal" (42) after staying at "the best hotel in Dover" (41) or the general contempt for the "incompetence" of the French (103), this concern with the markers of status may also suggest a characteristically English awareness of class. The name "Car-stairs" itself indicates both lower-middle-class limitation and the desire for upward mobility.

As a result, the Spillane theme of "hostility toward the sinful city with its corrupt men of wealth" (Cawelti 190) is largely translated in the British context into a passionate hatred for Establishment types: A "fat old dodderer with three chins and a crumpled suit. A middle-aged lady in a ridiculous hat . . . and . . . a chinless wonder who was probably a local politician" (163). By the time of the novel and in the wake of the Profumo, Philby and other scandals, distrust of politicians in Britain was widespread. A 1973 survey indicated that 65 percent of the British populace agreed with the statement "public officials don't care much about what people like me think,"[15] and Carstairs, upon reading of new scandals, observes with equal skepticism that "everyone's at it" (46). Where the trail of evil in the hard-boiled detective novel inevitably "leads back to the rich and respectable levels of society" (Cawelti 148), so too, in *The Big Needle,* all roads lead back to the Establishment and to John St. Clair Robins, Junior Minister at the Foreign Office, a man with a plummy accent and a perfect set of false teeth, and an individual who had ignored Carstairs when he was disguised as a workman (75).

Anthony Birch, in his text *The British System of Government* (1993), argues that it is helpful to think of British political culture as "fragmented" rather than as "either having collapsed or as being substantially unchanged." Certain segments of the society were by the 1970s "anything but deferential," and he points to students, ex-students, and trade unionists as obvious examples.[16] Alternatively, the rise of a small meritocracy in the 1960s and 1970s, and the resultant opportunities for personal achievement, have perhaps complicated British attitudes toward wealth and social standing. At the same time that Follett was a student radical, he dreamt of becoming "a captain of industry" or "a hot-shot journalist,"[17] and these mixed feelings toward materialism and living in "the American age" are present in *The Big Needle.*

Although a sympathetic character in the novel despises "the shallow social life led by many rich men's daughters" (120), Carstairs himself enjoys entrée to all the right parties. Once there, in front of the home of the man who had snubbed him when he was dressed as a plumber, he seems to derive satisfaction from the knowledge that birds have defecated on the stone lions guarding the estate (122). Apparently resentful of having been patronized by Robins, Carstairs is still capable of an equal condescension toward a Welsh garage boy. He states: "I would occasionally let him drive [my Ferrari], for which he worshipped me" (143).

This ambivalence toward wealth is a hallmark of the age. As we have seen, many people in Britain questioned the long-term benefits of adopting "American" values of conspicuous consumption and of individual self-gratification, a resistance that goes back at least to Graham Greene's famous diatribe against Hollywood, with its "gleaming lunch-bar-chromium version" of reality, "vulgar as only the great New World can be."[18] In *The Big Needle,* Carstairs listens attentively as a hitchhiker explains that "[a]dvertising is how American businessmen control the American people. And that's not just my theory—that's what they teach you in business school. I tell you, in the brainwashing field we are so far ahead of the Russians" (42). This standard British criticism of the intrusiveness and "vulgarity" of American life would recur in Follett's industrial espionage novels (analyzed in the next chapter) and would remain an aspect in as recent a novel as *The Third Twin.*

But in this early work, the conflict over American encroachments into British life represents both an attraction toward its popular culture, and a movement away from it toward more inherently British forms: the spy as dragon-slayer found in the heroic adventures of John Buchan, Sax Rohmer, and later, in Ian Fleming; the spy as predator and prey in the works of Eric Ambler, Geoffrey Household, and Graham Greene.

Although the first and second generations of British espionage writers can be distinguished by the amateur or professional status of the spy, these works in general stand in contrast to the American hard-boiled thriller where the detective is almost always an outsider, the search is contained within a single corrupt locus, and the pattern is the night journey leading to the encounter with the source of evil. In essence, the American thriller takes its tone and theme from a sense of betrayal, from the Puritan's anger that his covenant with God has somehow been broken and from his awareness that the world is the great wrong place.

British espionage heroes, at least as developed in the years prior to Follett's formative reading, are almost always connected to the society either as members of an Oxbridge circle (this is certainly the case in Le Queux's *Secrets of the Foreign Office* [1903], Childer's *Riddle of the Sands* [1903], and McNeile's *Bulldog Drummond* series) or as professionals within the Intelligence community. Although Maugham's *Ashen-*

don (1928), Greene's Scobie in *The Heart of the Matter* (1948), and Household's anonymous avenger in *Rogue Male* (1939) range in attitude from faint cynicism to despair to outrage, they are still men of breeding, education and, as Household puts it, belong to Class X, which he defines indirectly as a group whose primary loyalties are in the English country-side and who take on positions of leadership out of obligation rather than financial need.[19]

In addition, the setting of the British thriller tends to be interna-tional, rather than restricted to a single brutal city, and the chase across various regions or countries helps define the form in works ranging from Buchan's *The Thirty-Nine Steps* (1915), to Ian Fleming's *On Her Majesty's Secret Service* (1963), to Helen MacInnes' *Snare of the Hunter* (1975), to as recent a work as Jeffrey Archer's *A Matter of Honor* (1986). The chase, or the hunt, figures prominently as a plot pattern, with the classic reversal in many books written during the inter-war years of the hunted turning on his foes and becoming a hunter instead. The Puritan allegory which infuses these British tales is John Bunyan's *The Pilgrim's Progress* where Christian is sorely tested but reaches the Celestial City after all.[20]

Follett's *The Big Needle* shows its indebtedness to these more British forms through parallels to both the book and the Hitchcock film version of *The Thirty-Nine Steps*. In the first place, the film's stern and pious Scottish crofter and his more tolerant wife are turned in *The Big Needle* into a Welsh farm woman who is "rather more jolly than her [Nonconformist] husband" (139), and the novel's chase across a number of locations until all points converge upon the sea here becomes a race from London to Paris to the west coast of Wales.

Second, the hunter/hunted motif from later British works figures prominently in the text. Toward the end of the novel, Carstairs turns upon his enemy who believes he has won "the game" (168). Moments later, Carstairs springs "the trap" (169) and defeats his adversary, thus restoring order to the society in ways that would elude a Phillip Mar-lowe, whose discovery in each novel is that evil is endemic and endur-ing. Though the nouveau riche Carstairs has also been used to reflect certain class resentments, in the very last lines of the novel he seems reconnected to the society in a very British way: "I'm going to live . . . on the farm," he declares. "I could do with a year or two of doing noth-ing, too. I shall paint" (175), thus re-establishing his credentials as a man of leisure and a gentleman whose true heritage is in the countryside.

Follett's first published work remains distinctly British in one other important way: how pace is often secondary to the poetic qualities of language. Despite the approximation of American tough-guy slang and its resultant rapidity of actions, Follett occasionally halts the storyline completely for the sake of literary reflectiveness:

The Thames never fails to soothe me. It's [a] grey, slow river with dirty grey buildings on either side, and even in bright sunlight it never seems to sparkle like rivers are supposed to. It's a good river for suicides, speaking of oblivion in the low sweep of its murky depths. . . . The speed of the river hardly alters in hundreds of years, unmoved by the increasingly frenetic pace of life all around it. (85-86)

While this may be the atmospheric equivalent of Mickey Spillane's rainy New York, it seems equally akin to Joseph Conrad's "great spirit of the past upon the lower reaches of the Thames" or to late Le Carré's "a dark sea rain [that] had enveloped Pym's England" and to other increasingly dense depictions of place. Even when describing brutality, in passages that for the most part retain the American style, a more mellifluous rhetoric sometimes creeps into *The Big Needle,* as in the artful repetitions and the alliteration in the following: "I brought the spanner down again and again in his face, my right arm a mindless machine operated by blind, consuming rage" (130)—a passage in part reminiscent of Tennyson.[21]

The competing cultural, political and literary influences in *The Big Needle* are not always successfully reconciled, and Follett has observed that his early works are not effectively paced. Toward the end of the novel, and in part because of the abandonment of formula, the story relies increasingly on explanation rather than on action to tie-up all the loose ends. The solution of the mystery, in fact, comes in the form of a dream—an element more from drug literature than from either classical or hard-boiled detective fiction. On the other hand, Follett has also stated that the book "wasn't all that bad [and] I'm not ashamed of it." By incorporating strong chapter hooks and interrelated actions, Follett had written something that would sell: "If you can tell a story and not bore anybody, and keep it simple," he has noted about his early writing efforts, "you'll get published. That whole business about luck and fate doesn't apply; it's just a myth."[22]

More importantly, he was learning what Alfred Hitchcock had known since the 1930s: that mixing together "generic elements from [various sources] in a blend . . . would guarantee their appeal to audiences."[23] Although John Le Carré had shown the possibilities of combining detective, espionage and mainstream literary elements into a single text, his movement has been increasingly toward the post-modern experiment and away from genre fiction. Follett's earliest novel instead represents an interest in mixing different types of formulas, a technique he would perfect in *Eye of the Needle,* where he blends elements from the women's category romance with ingredients from the male-oriented espionage thriller, and where he balances melodrama against literary texture, thus showing that the mainstream novel can be considered merely another genre. In addition, *The Big Needle* represents the kind of transatlantic cross-fertilization that has been taking place between British and American popular culture for some time.

Even though much of this chapter has focused on likely American cultural influences on a British writer such as Follett, and his tentative resistance to them, *"cross-*fertilization" does remain a valid analogy. In later years, Follett would begin to recognize that a "secret agent in enemy territory is probably the most reliable of all scenarios for a novel of suspense,"[24] and when he would begin to follow these more classic British thriller lines, and yet make them resonate with an American readership, his international success was assured.

3

THE "MYSTERY" OF EARLY SUCCESS

A stroll through a London bookstore confirms Follett's observation that he sells many more books in the United States than he does in his own country. "I do better in Italy, even," he has said, and while entire bookshop shelves in England seem devoted to Jeffrey Archer or to Len Deighton, only two or three of Follett's seventeen-plus novels appear to be in stock and find a narrow place somewhere between the collected works of James Follett, a BBC television writer, and the thrillers of Frederick Forsyth. "Naturally, I think the Americans are right," Follett has quipped,[1] but a study of the first two novels written under his own name—*The Shakeout* (1975) and *The Bear Raid* (1976)—indicates that early in his career Follett was still attempting to please a mainstream British readership and was writing in the vein of the social realist novels of the 1950s, especially John Braine's *Room at the Top* (1957).

As we have seen, prior to these two works, Follett had used the pseudonym "Symon Myles" to publish a series of hard-boiled mysteries—*The Big Needle, The Big Black,* and *The Big Hit*—written at the rate of one every four to five months in 1974-1975, while he himself was still in his early twenties,[2] and from 1975-1978 was also writing children's stories, science fiction books, and crime capers under three separate pen names—"Martin Martinsen," "Bernard L. Ross," and "Zachary Stone"—one for each of the categories.

In an interview with the *Toronto Star,* Follett admitted that his hard-boiled mysteries were weak: *The Big Needle* "has a great deal of gratuitous sex and violence and it's not very well structured," and elsewhere he has stated that the majority of the works he wrote during his "literary apprenticeship" came out under pseudonyms because his agent felt he would write better books later in his life.[3] Follett, in fact, made rapid progress in his craft: the same year that the last of *The Big* mysteries was published—1975—*The Shakeout* appeared. "I had learned to respect my material," Follett has stated. "In my development as a writer they mark a place half way between bad and good."[4] As we shall see, they mark a juncture in other ways as well and may essentially represent "the road untaken."

That Follett, as a recent University of London graduate working as a journalist, should have been drawn to the thriller form in the 1970s is not surprising. During the Cold War, that genre probably provided the most immediate publishing opportunities for an aspiring novelist. As John Cawelti and Bruce Rosenberg have pointed out, by the 1980s the spy hero had become the paramount protagonist of a major form of mass-market literature, "increasingly replacing earlier popular heroic figures like the cowboy and the hardboiled detective."[5] Moreover, in the same way that Graham Greene's childhood reading of popular writers such as H. Rider Haggard, Marjorie Bowen, and Stanley Weyman proved formative, so too, Follett's youthful interest in Edgar Rice Burroughs, Daphne Du Maurier, and Ian Fleming[6] may have prepared him for the writing of a certain kind of work.

But throughout the 1970s in Britain, another kind of literary model would have been inescapable for any ambitious beginning writer: the phenomenal success of first-time novelist John Braine, whose *Room at the Top* "received attention as a serious contribution to the 'English Novel' and became a mass bestseller to rival Ian Fleming's James Bond thrillers."[7]

In it, and in the less-successful sequel *Life at the Top* (1962), Braine focused on the moral dilemma of one Joe Lampton, a kind of Everyman in the midst of post-war British materialism, who must also choose between Goods and Good Deeds—in *Room at the Top,* a choice represented by a marriage of convenience or a marriage of the heart. In its thirtieth reprint by 1981, and examining such social issues as class and regional divisions, *Room at the Top* quite obviously spoke to some particularly British concerns and posed some especially poignant post-war questions: what is the price of affluence or power in the late twentieth century? How "modern" and therefore "Americanized" should the nation be?

These novels combined a realist style with strong plot considerations. We can find similar approaches, issues, and even story elements in Follett's two industrial espionage novels, which become an interesting, if not always seamless, cross-stitching of the Buchanesque and the Social Realist.

John Buchan's contribution to the spy novel has already been noted. In works such as *Greenmantle* (1916) and *Mr. Standfast* (1919), Buchan established the basic formulaic patterns of the heroic spy novel and emphasized the importance of the chase, or hurried flight and pursuit across an exotic landscape, as one of the genre's central elements. Cawelti and Rosenberg point to Sax Rohmer's *Fu Manchu* novels, Ambler's *Mask of Dimitrios* (1939), Hitchcock's "The Lady Vanishes"

(1938), Greene's *Orient Express* (1932), several of the James Bond stories, and Le Carré's *The Spy Who Came in From the Cold* (1965) as works which attest to the dominance of Buchan's plotlines.[8] Buchan has also been cited for his allegorical use of coincidence and for the absence of believable, complete female characters. As we shall see, Follett would struggle with these and other aspects of his literary inheritance.

Having already written three mysteries by the mid-1970s and determined to distinguish himself from other espionage novelists, Follett chose to write about "an unconventional subject—industrial espionage"[9]—a decision which he termed "quite a good notion" and part of his attempt to write "a better novel" (*SK* i).

Despite this goal of originality, however, various formulaic elements from the political spy genre inhabit both *The Shakeout* and *The Bear Raid*. In numerous spy novels written after the war, such as Ted Allebury's *A Choice of Enemies* (1973), the spy comes from the Oxbridge network but has cut his teeth in military intelligence. Here, too, Follett's Piers Roper has spent "three years at Oxford and five in Army Intelligence" (*SK* 32). Another plot device dating back to Buchan but used frequently by Le Carré is the search for the mole who wears the mask of English respectability. In *The Thirty-Nine Steps,* the German spies pretend to be "three ordinary, game-playing suburban Englishmen, wearisome, if you like, but sordidly innocent"; in Le Carré's *Tinker, Tailor, Soldier, Spy,* published the year before *The Shakeout,* the traitor is the most English of the lot, a "model . . . , inspiration [and] torch-bearer of a certain kind of . . . English calling,"[10] and thus, the least likely suspect. In Follett's *The Shakeout,* the mole lives in a "select suburb" across from "a small pub with a large yard" and appears thoroughly above suspicion because of the markers of respectability: membership in a golf club, ownership of a Jaguar, and the wearing of the suburban uniform: "slacks and a knitted cardigan" (140). In addition, Follett makes use of a James Bond-like struggle against a hallucinogen injected into the spy's system to make him talk,[11] as well as formulaic narrative hooks such as a sensuous and pliant female at the end of each first chapter. In both of these early novels, the vamp makes herself available to the spy/hero, Piers Roper, who is, as per the genre, a dour sybarite and member of Clubland.

Richard Usborne, in his study of spy writers from the first two decades of the 20th century, coined the term "clubland heroes" to demonstrate that Buchan's Richard Hannay, McNiele's Bulldog Drummond and Dornford Yates' Jonah Mansel all shared strong attachments to the English countryside (their real home) and belonged to city clubs out of the need to reaffirm their genteel status when in town. As such, these agents could remain amateurs and gentlemen despite taking on a variety of assignments. David Cannadine, in his article "James Bond and the Decline of England," has further established that Ian Fleming created a latter-day clubland hero who pines for the days of Richard Hannay, frequently threatens to quit the organization, and immerses himself in the nearest contemporary equivalent of the gentleman's club—the casino.[12]

Nostalgia for the "antiquated romanticism" of the past, as John Le Carré put it, that trained an individual "to rule, divide and conquer . . . [when] the reality was a poor island,"[13] was treated as a tragic flaw in *Tinker, Tailor, Soldier, Spy;* Len Deighton's protagonist in *Yesterday's Spy* (1976) also recognizes that the old verities have been pushed aside in a world of push-button technology and treachery. But Piers Roper's nostalgia seems quintessential Bond. He laments the passing of "the old breed of London taxi-drivers" (*SK* 25), disapproves of the use of new ten-pence coins instead of shillings in public telephones (14), and dislikes polystyrene as a packing material (26). In fact, Piers Roper, like James Bond, seems happiest when he is safely ensconced in "the smoking-room at his club" (20), or can savor a particular wine before slicing into a steak and watching "the juices from its rare center swirl and darken in the gravy" (6). This sort of projection, as we have seen, from lower-middle-class actuality to an upper-middle-class persona, was tentatively established in *The Big Needle,* but with the sometimes confusing admixture of counterculture politics. Here, the New Left outlook is dispensed with, and Follett adopts the outward expression of conservative attitudes as one more ingredient in the making of the espionage story.

This Tory mask appears elsewhere: in Piers' preference for smoking "Senior Service, an unmistakeably English cigarette" (*BR* 73), which is perhaps an attempt to make him, like Oppenheim's Hardcross Courage and other Clubland heroes, "Saxon to the backbone;"[14] in his capital city snobbery toward the provinces: "London was home, the rest of the country a strange land" (*SK* 59), and in the anti-American sniping reminiscent of James Bond's air of superiority

In Follett's *The Bear Raid,* as in Fleming's *Diamonds Are Forever* (also set largely in the United States), negative stereotypes of Americans are prevalent. Such stereotypes would occasionally recur in Follett's later works, such as *Capricorn One* or *The Third Twin,* but the anti-American criticism is particularly pointed in these two early novels. American cuisine, for example, is deplorable (*BR* 8); the conversation is "loud" and "rapid" (47), and the clothing is "fractionally out-of-date" in a way that seems "typically American" (52). Worse still, American businessmen are pushy (56), have "style without taste" (75), and favor "mustard coloured suit[s] and . . . loud tie[s]" (77). When Americans speak it is remarkable if their pronunciation is "a little more correct than the usual" (86). They either say "Lemme putchon hold, okay?" (123) or "nope" (*SK* 154), prompting Piers Roper to comment that an American businessman talks "like a character out of 'Gunfight at the O.K. Corral'" (154). One wonders if gangster movies and cowboy films did, in fact, form the basis for these stereotypes,[15] since other inaccuracies occur, such as referring to a Detroit suburb as "Hamtrack" (*BR* 54) instead of "Hamtramck" or describing Detroit's Gratiot Avenue—even the Gratiot Avenue of twenty-five years ago—as heavy with traffic, where "all the cars looked new and expensive" (46).

Graham Greene's notorious anti-Americanism has been assessed as "really an extension of his dislike for the suburban Protestant materialism of England,"[16] and it is tempting to suggest that for Follett, too, the dilemma concerning what constitutes "the good life" in Britain was being transferred onto an even more consumer-oriented society—the United States.

Follett's own attitudes toward the morality of affluence have, of course, become complicated as he himself has become more financially successful and has come to a first-hand understanding of the American reader and of American life. He was fascinated, for example, by the prosperity of Dallas, which he visited in the 1980s, and was intrigued by Ross Perot, who had also become a millionaire while still young.[17] But in the 1970s, when Follett was writing *The Shakeout* and *The Bear Raid,* a concern with the limitations of wealth was sharply expressed. Writing under the pseudonym "Bernard L. Ross," for example, he referred to Houston as a city "with no class at all" (*Capricorn* 7), and in *The Modigliani Scandal* (1976) has a character comment that "it's a scandal that there should be anyone" qualified to go to the university but who has "to stay home and work in a factory . . . while there are people earning what you and I earn" (73). Even in the children's story *The Power Twins* (1976), the hero realizes that "the good life" has its limitations: his quarters, which look "just like a posh hotel" appear to him "like a jail."[18]

Filled with skepticism toward corrupt business practices and "the League of Life [, which] is paid by Unilon Makers to make trouble for the Worm World" (64), this, and his other writings from the mid-1970s reflect the kind of social criticism leveled by observers such as David Craig, who noted that the British literary protest of the post-war period:

. . . is often expressed as a critique of affluence. The "private affluence" of large wage-packet and easy credit . . . has been reached by a road—the mixed economy—which allows deep inequalities, the patchiest kind of improvements, and a flourishing of rackets (Rachman-type landlords, clubs run by crooks on American lines) which almost advertise the attractions of getting rich quick by the most anti-social means.[19]

Clearly, the anti-American attitudes in *The Shakeout* and *The Bear Raid* are both formulaic, since it is Bond who in *Diamonds Are Forever* confronts and defeats the Spangled Mob, something which the Americans have been too timid or incompetent to accomplish for themselves, as well as Social Realist: the answer to the question how modern and affluent to be in the post-war period becomes "not modern at all" if it means drowning in American-style materialism. ("'You have old-fashioned tastes,'" Piers is told in *The Shakeout* [11], and appears not unhappy with this assessment. In *The Bear Raid* he makes note of the expensive clutter representing decadence in a "typical" American suburban home: "the electric carving knife and the magnetized can opener. A glossy art book. . . , the spotless open fireplace . . . and the inevitable portable TV" [74].)

On more than one occasion Follett has demurred that he is "not an original writer. I'm very derivative."[20] But what has always been original in his work has been his ability to draw from and blend different *kinds* of sources. Early or late, Follett has been able to target diverse segments of the book-buying public by incorporating themes and motifs from a wide variety of literary categories.

As indicated above, Follett's indebtedness to another kind of English novel, the "Movement" novels of Kingsley Amis and John Wain, and to the "Angry" writers of the 1950s—John Osborne and Colin Wilson—is particularly salient in that *The Shakeout* and *The Bear Raid* contain numerous similarities to that high-water mark of British social realism: John Braine's *Room at the Top*. As we have seen, Braine's two works were in the forefront of British public consciousness, having become "a relatively unusual publishing phenomenon, being both an instant bestseller and able to command regular reprints for a period of [over] twenty-five years."[21] In fact, not only had the two books been made into films in the 1960s, as had other popular social realist works, but by the early 1970s, the time during which Ken Follett was constructing the two Piers Roper novels, Braine's *Room*—and *Life at the Top* had been combined into a popular British television series, spurring additional sales of the Penguin reprint.

In Follett's two Piers Roper mysteries we find, firstly, a more complicated class-consciousness than was present in *The Big Needle;* it is now more akin to the attitudes expressed by Braine's Joe Lampton, where the individual who has moved into a higher social circle fears that he is constantly being assessed: "If he had drunk soup with a dessert spoon, or tasted his wine before the meat was served, he would have revealed himself to be socially clumsy" (*SK* 45). At the same time, he constantly assesses those beneath him:

So what about Monica? She talked, dressed, and walked like a debutante, but Piers knew it was phoney . . . her accent owed more to Rotherhithe than Roedean . . . and [he] hoped her vocabulary wasn't infectious. (*BR* 17)

In the above example, accent is used to reaffirm Pier's social superiority over Monica, but accent, the most immediate indicator of status in Britain, can also be used deliberately to show working-class or regional identification. In Follett's *The Power Twins,* a children's novel published in 1976—the same year as *The Bear Raid*—a member of the *lumpenproletariat* on a distant planet proudly explains that "I come up again pretty rapid, I can tell you. Them Worms could've ate me, unit and all. . . . Lucky I could see 'em" (53), and in *The Modigliani Scandal,* also published the same year, a character on the fringes of the art world happily terms himself the "[t]oken working class representative" and intentionally "broadened his London accent" for sardonic effect while at a society party (75). In these examples, accent is being used to emphasize the favorable self-image held by certain groups: the regional worker, whose warm, decent qualities are revealed in the use of a local dialect; the Cockney, with his fast and amusing slang, who is the salt of the earth. Assessing the "New Literature" in England since the war, David Craig asserted that social realist writers unfold everyday experience "in its own language, the speech of the characters themselves, rather than the standard English of a detached observer as in most literature hitherto." But in a number of examples from the fiction of the time, dialect stresses the gulf of class and is used instead as a weapon: Joe Lampton, in *Room at the Top,* decides to drop "into broad Yorkshire to counterattack [Jack] Wale's genuine officer's accent, as carelessly correct as his tweed suit."[22]

This perception of class and accent is one noteworthy similarity between Follett's novels from the 1970s, especially *The Shakeout* and *The Bear Raid,* and works such as Braine's *Room*—and *Life at the Top.* In addition, there is the moral dilemma faced by both Piers Roper and Joe Lampton. If Joe is the Everyman whose choice is "effectively between social values and authentic human ones,"[23] then Piers, like the Piers Plowman of the 14th-century allegory, also encounters a corrupt world and can only redeem it—and himself—through social concern, an effort which ultimately fails.

Initially, both Joe and Piers are self-interested manipulators of other people: "Piers made up his mind that he would use her" (*SK* 64), but fall genuinely in love with the women they are trying to exploit. Old training is hard to break, however, and ultimately Piers, like Joe, selects money and position over love, realizing too late that he has "done everything well, and nothing good" (*SK* 129) and that his emotional future without Anne will be a "perpetual motion of the waves," "a faint fizz" in a puddle, and dreams "scattered in the air like so much pathetic flotsam" (157).

Follett, who would later be noted for a "clean and purposeful prose" and for his general avoidance of literary "metaphor and allusion"[24] is, in this early work, quite obviously relying on the more mainstream literary technique of figurative language and descriptive passages. These two Piers Roper novels, in fact, seem to alternate between the "clean and purposeful prose" of the popular suspense novel, with its combination of dialogue and staging: "'Lucky you.' Her lipstick smeared the glass as she drank" (*BR* 42), and langourously descriptive paragraphs, replete with simile or personification: "The white flakes had looked attractive as they meandered past his twelfth-floor office window, blissfully ignorant of the mucky fate that awaited them underneath the shoes of City commuters" (*SK* 24).

Just as in *The Big Needle*, where the burden of the book was to tell two types of stories—the counterculture experience and the hard-boiled detective tale—here, too, the Piers Roper novels labor under the necessity of alternating between two different genres—the chase melodrama and the drama of a deepening personal awareness. Although a Buchanesque trajectory exists in both novels, with the chase from city to suburb to factory town in *The Shakeout* and from London to Detroit to New York in *The Bear Raid,* the pace is considerably slowed down because of the apparent interest in developing character, an indication that in Follett's later "apprenticeship" novels he was striving to create portraits of "flawed, struggling human beings who undergo personal torment, pain and deprivation."[25] It is in this attempt at character complexity, at a psychological complicatedness achieved in part through the blending of literary categories, that Follett was best able to breathe new life into an old form.

Piers, in *The Shakeout,* is an individual of highly developed sensibilities who listens to Mahler and collects fine art, but who doesn't "want to fall in love. It's messy and emotional," he says, "and I'm not very good at it" (30). Astute at playing the organizational game, he realizes that the problem "was Life as a Whole" (127) and becomes, in essence, James Bond with the private *weltschmerz* of a Joe Lampton. In an article written a few years later in which he discussed the necessity of character development in spy novels, Follett observed that on "the surface [the spy] is tough; underneath he is vulnerable" and that "one of the attractions of reading about spies is that a spy's public image is an extreme case of the kind of false front we all put on from time to time."[26] By depicting genuinely conflicted individuals, Follett was thus able to move beyond the stock figure of the clandestine agent toward an almost ancient Greek sense of heroes: protagonists who are appealing in part because they are fallible and are enmeshed in moral dilemmas.

In his later, perhaps more fully integrated works, Follett would make the spy the *villain* of the story rather than the hero but would retain a sympathetic understanding for them as well as create "credible motives and understandable passions." As Follett mentioned in an interview, "'If you're a novelist you have to be able to empathize with people who are not like you,'" and his later novels would be cited for a "special sensitivity towards female characters," and an ability to "realistically [portray] women who have led fairly ordinary lives but are capable of heroics when needed,"[27] comments which apply to subsequent novels such as *Eye of the Needle, The Man from St. Petersburg, Lie Down with Lions,* and *The Third Twin.*

His artistic development from *The Big* mysteries to his industrial espionage novels is in part evidenced by the way in which women characters are depicted: rather than being the one-dimensional sex partners of his first novel, the women characters now contain some of the "centrality and strength" which he has termed "the only thing I've ever done which comes close to being original."[28]

In fact, in these two early works from the 1970s, Follett appears to play deliberately against the stereotypical depiction of women present either in Clubland spy novels or in much post-war thriller fiction.

In *The Shakeout,* for example, Anne's robust appetite while eating seems a conscious effort to reverse standard sexual roles: "[S]he polished off a huge steak and a jacket potato while *he* toyed with breast of turkey and green salad" (82 [emphasis added]). Later, she swallows her "drink in one gulp" (83), takes him out to a rock concert (97), and sensitizes him to social and political issues, saying "[W]hat would you know about the way police treat black people" (91). Where the sequel *The Bear Raid* is less successful is in this very area of complex characterization, a criticism leveled against Braine's sequel to *Room at the Top* as well: "The most serious failure in [*Life at the Top*] is Joe Lampton. He's never a character, he's an attitude. Surely nobody's psyche—top, bottom, or middle—is compounded entirely of class problems."[29] Piers Roper's psyche in *The Bear Raid* is expressed through contrived stream-of-consciousness flashbacks, the occasional sexual qualm, and grudging resentments toward

America. And perhaps because the love interest is now an American woman, the depiction seems less certain. We know relatively little about her and for two-thirds of the book she is referred to as "the girl" rather than by name. Her dialogue is equally lifeless as when she tries to sympathize with Piers' unhappiness by saying, "'It passes. . . . Believe me, Piers, it passes'" and he replies, "'I believe you,'" before the italicized interior monologue, *"But there will always be a small scar"* (66).

These two books did not sell particularly well. Apparently, Follett had not yet learned that "American bookbuyers [would] make me rich and famous" and that each of his paperback books in print today would sell only 5,000 copies per year in Britain compared with 50,000 copies per year in the United States. Perhaps his aspiration was still to write the "long English paper," as his first American publisher put it,[30] or, at the very least, to win acceptance from a home audience. During the 1980s, Follett at times indicated some dismay over his relatively low sales in Britain, and even today feels "[t]here's a lot of the market still to conquer. I want people to know who I am."[31]

In his later novels, Follett would start to make a deliberate shift by catering to more American tastes and would become more restrained in his criticism of "the vulgarity" of American life. His very experimentation in other genres such as science fiction, children's stories, and crime capers under a number of pseudonyms, as well as his work in nonfiction and television, suggest his willingness to move on to other stages of development. Quite early in his career he remarked on his desire to work in genres other than the thriller,[32] and he no doubt realized after the publication of *The Shakeout* and *The Bear Raid* that he had carried these various artistic experiments as far as he could at that time. Presumably, there seemed little point in developing a *series* of Piers Roper novels since, by his own admission, "Roper is only a sketch of a character, a hasty drawing with an unfinished feel to it" (*SK* ii). Worse still, the very effort to distinguish himself by writing on industrial espionage may have been self-limiting: "The fate of the world may hang on the work of a James Bond or a Smiley," Follett commented years later, "but it is hard for a reader to become emotionally involved in the theft of industrial secrets" (*SK* ii).

Nevertheless, these various lessons would be put to good use in a subsequent thriller—*Eye of the Needle*—published two years later; a work in which Follett, like Braine, would be able to fully integrate the popular and the serious and which would lead to a place on bookshop shelves around the world. Through an examination of Ken Follett's apprenticeship novels, the "mystery" of his early success can be solved: *Eye of the Needle* was a success which was six years in coming and the result of considerable effort and experimentation.

4

AN EYE FOR LITERATURE

Henry Faber, a Nazi spy under deep cover, determines that the Allied invasion plans for 1944 involve a deception. Hurrying to return to Germany, Faber is tracked down by the spycatcher, Professor Godliman, and his assistant from Special Branch, Frederick Bloggs. Faber is killed on a remote island in the North Sea where he has taken refuge and has had a brief love affair with Lucy Rose, a woman who is married to a crippled R.A.F. pilot.

"The plot of *Eye of the Needle* is of course very simple," Follett stated in the introduction to a reprinted apprenticeship novel. "[I]n fact, it can be written down in three paragraphs, as indeed I did write it when I first thought of it."[1]

By the mid-1970s, Follett had moved from newspaper work to the editorial department of Everest Books, where he eventually became deputy managing director and had already published eleven "apprenticeship" novels, mostly under a variety of pseudonyms. At a book publishers' convention, Anthony Cheetham, the managing director of Futura Publications, suggested to Follett that he write a World War II adventure novel. Thirty years had passed since the invasion of Normandy and previously classified information regarding British deception plans and Nazi efforts to uncover them was now available to the public, information which Follett had apparently read.[2] After a night on the town with other publishing executives, Follett wrote his three-paragraph plot synopsis of a loner spy in England who finally discovers a gigantic Allied invasion hoax in the South of England and who attempts to return to Germany.

The premise struck Follett as a bestselling idea. He had read Frederick Forsyth's *Day of the Jackal* to see why it had sold so many copies. "I realized I was writing with the wrong attitude. . . . I had to know more, be more attentive to detail."[3] He may have also recognized that a Forsyth-like telescoping plot could be used to tell a love story in combination with an adventure tale; what he later saw as a turning point in the thriller form since for the first time it could include a strong female character. Cheetham, who had already published two of Follett's books, recognized the potential in the idea as well, but lost the synopsis. Follett, however, was fortunately able to remember enough of the story to begin work,[4] and received a commission. Three months later, *Eye of the Needle* was finished. "I knew it was a terrific book," Follett has said,[5] and after an intensive marketing campaign the novel started to appear on the best-seller lists several weeks before the official publication date. The first two editions alone sold over 10 million copies worldwide and film rights were sold to United Artists that same year—1978.[6]

Critical reaction to *Eye of the Needle* was almost entirely favorable. Lauded by Roderick MacLeish of the *Washington Post* as "quite simply the best spy novel to come out of England in years," it was a Literary Guild selection and winner of the Edgar Allan Poe Award from the Mystery Writers of America. A *Time* reviewer praised Follett's plotting skills as well as his "nicely crafted, three-dimensional figures who linger in the memory long after the circumstances blur." Richard Freedman of the *New York Times* called the book "visceral and intellectual," while Peter S. Prescott, in one of the few unfavorable reviews, did observe that the novel improved upon *Day of the Jackal* "by virtue of its remarkable pace, its astute use of violence [and] its sense of particular environments."[7]

In sum, *Eye of the Needle* can be considered a work of significant literary quality with broad reader appeal—a novel which both "entertains and instructs."

The goal of entertaining while instructing, or of writing intelligently for a mass audience, was one faced by other post-war British writers such as Graham Greene, Kingsley Amis or John Le Carré who also turned to espionage fiction as a form with sufficient flexibility to allow for good storytelling and the incorporation of ideas.

"[A]fter the publication of James Joyce's *Ulysses* in 1922," Follett pointed out in an essay written shortly after the success of *Eye of the Needle,* "introspection became the paramount literary technique," resulting in little more than "thoughtful tedium" about "the trivia of [upper] middle-class life." If Modernist experiments in Britain had largely run their course by mid-century, his essay suggests, the contemporary novel could be reinvigorated by returning to its 19th-century origins in melodrama (and, by implication, the earlier heritage of allegory). "Revolution, tragedy, passion, power, death: Thomas Hardy and Emily Brontë could write about these." The same "virtues we expect of serious fiction [can give us] mass-market success."[8]

In many ways a traditional novel, *Eye of the Needle* follows E. M. Forster's precept that a novel should focus on marriage, mores, manners, and money. Not only do we find precise details of ordinary life—"Faber spread margarine thinly on a slice of wholemeal bread, and momentarily yearned for a fat sausage" (5), but an interest in the social rites and rituals of a broad cross-section of English life—"[David] came from precisely the same social stratum of society as they did. Father thought he was a shade too opinionated, but mother said the landed gentry had been saying that about undergraduates for six hundred years" (23).

In other ways, it is an historical novel written by "an author young enough indeed [not] to have known wartime days,"[9] but full of the period details and period attitudes needed to create an era's verisimilitude. For example, when Lucy examines herself in a mirror, her 1940s outfit is described, but more importantly, her 1940s outlook is as well: "It would not have been right to go away gorgeously dressed this year; but she felt she had achieved the kind of briskly practical, yet attractive look that was rapidly becoming fashionable" (26).

At times this historical view, this nostalgia, may result in a slight distortion of the past, in the fond view of the English as they would like to remember themselves during the war, singing and able to "take it." But Tom Harrison, in *Living through the Blitz,* points to many instances of panic, desperation and public fear and "a cover-up of the more disagreeable facts."[10]

If the retrospective view is a simplifying one, it does allow for an older, more self-consciously literary style than one might find in a standard thriller; in artful repetitions to establish a character's emotional life—

She heard him scrape across the floor, heard the bed creak as he hauled himself on to it, heard his clothes hit the corner of the room as he undressed, then heard the final groaning of the springs as he lay down and pulled the blankets up over him. (44)

—or in metaphor used for the same purpose: "Crossing the beach the wave would rise even higher, its crest curling in a question mark" (174). This older literary style is combined with the occasional Modernist influence, especially center-of-consciousness point-of-view, or dream imagery.

But the passages dealing with Lucy or the island she lives on seem the most deliberately literary, establishing a pastoral "little England" ("two happy, handsome people, children of solid, comfortably off, backbone-of-England-type families getting married in a country church in the finest summer weather Britain can offer" [21]), and sometimes engaging in a lush descriptiveness, reminiscent of 19th-century travel writing:

The higher land is ruled by heather. Every few years the man—yes, there is a man here—sets fire to the heather, and then the grass will grow and the sheep can graze here too; but after a couple of years the heather comes back, God knows from where, and drives the sheep away until the man burns it again. (38)

In fact, this return to an earlier travelogue and historical style allows Follett to resurrect the pre-Modernist omniscient narrator, as in the direct authorial comment in the above passage, or elsewhere:

[N]o jackboots sounded in the tiled choir in this August of 1940; not yet. The sun glowed through stained glass windows that had survived Cromwell's iconoclasts and Henry VIII's greed, and the roof resounded to the notes of an organ that had yet to yield to woodworm and dry rot. (20)

According to Roderick MacLeish, in his review of *Eye of the Needle,* this second-hand historical approach "flattens moral conjecture" and smooths out, for example, such useful "ambiguities and uncertainties that torment and glorify" first-hand accounts of war-time tensions. A counter-view holds that the voice of the historical narrator in Follett's *Eye of the Needle* results in the effective "trick of standing back and approaching things from a distance," the kind of authorial detachment which Wayne Booth points to as the essence of narrative.[11]

In other ways, too, *Eye of the Needle* takes on the feel and texture of the serious novel. Follett may have lamented the fact that in the early 20th century "character became the only permissible subject for a serious novel,"[12] but he has also indicated that in the canonical works of literature he admires, plot develops out of character and not the other way around:

The story must develop because of the choices made by the main characters. [The character] must not be a mere victim of events. . . . [If] we've ended up with a story about a moral dilemma . . . , this should not surprise us. Moral dilemmas have been the stuff of fiction since long before the novel was invented, let alone the thriller—think of Hamlet.[13]

This is, of course, one of the features of what is generally called "serious literature"—a complex and multi-dimensional characterization that is both "fictional" and "true to life."

An outgrowth in part of the reserved, but vulnerable Piers Roper character Follett had described in his two previous novels, Faber's characterization is enriched by showing his repulsion when killing, by demonstrating his contempt for the Nazi movement generally, and by detailing his background. Not only has Faber "led the life of a monk for seven years" (202) out of dedication to a higher purpose, but the reader finds out that his "father was the second son; so was Heinrich" and that he'd once broken the arm of his wrestling instructor (88).

"[In] creating character, I like to start with the person's parents," Follett observed, and the very focus on the character's exploits, his ordeal and quest, forces an identification where otherwise there might not be one. Follett recognized that it is therefore "possible for a character to be both hero and villain"—at least temporarily—if there are several layers to the individual's personality.[14]

But *Eye of the Needle* is also a formula spy story, with its chase across the Scottish moors, its series of encounters and escapes, and its hunter/hunted format. In popular literature, images of the "manhunt," or tracking down of the adversary, date back at least to Cooper's *The Deerslayer* (1841), and the concept of springing a trap on a tormentor can be found in Poe's "The Cask of Amontillado" (1846), in Conan Doyle's "The Adventure of The Speckled Band" (1892), or in Baroness Orczy's historical spy melodrama, *The Scarlet Pimpernel* (1905); but as a motif, the hunter/hunted reversal finds its fullest thematic expression in Richard Connell's famous short story "The Most Dangerous Game" (1924) and in the works of Geoffrey Household and Graham Greene. Household uses the "manhunt" in *Rogue Male* (1939) to explore aristocratic decadence on the eve of a world war; Greene uses such imagery in several novels to show that a man is pursued by guilt, or by God, or by an unwanted self.

By the 1940s, the spy/counterspy struggle was so ingrained in popular literature as to appear in Agatha Christie's *N or M?* (1941), Michael Innes' *The Secret Vanguard* (1940), and in several other anti-Nazi thrillers. By the 1960s, it had become enough of a cliché to be regularly spoofed in the comic book *Mad Magazine*.

Follett, however, is able to use the hunter/hunted motif, and other devices, in both a formulaic and a non-formulaic way. His boyhood reading of genre thrillers has already been commented on, and his adult interests have ranged from British adventure writer Dennis Wheatley to the poet and translator D. M. Thomas.[15] *Eye of the Needle,* too, remains a combination of the serious and the popular. In numerous sections, Follett makes reference to D. H. Lawrence; in others, he undercuts the formulaic elements of his work by mentioning Barbara Cartland, melodrama, or suspense movies. Stylistically, sections of lush, literary prose describing Lucy's point-of-view contrast with either filmic "quick-cuts" or with the short, lean, terse rhythms used for Henry's world:

[Faber] wondered what to do about the boat. Ideally, he would scuttle it, but he might be seen doing so. If he left it in a harbor somewhere, or simply moored at the canalside, the police would connect it with the murders that much sooner; and that would tell them in which direction he was moving. He postponed the decision. (110)

If at times the novel seems almost a pastiche from different sources—the spy novel, the war novel, the category romance, the detective film, the war history—Follett's thorough grounding in popular forms allows him to achieve character complexity in one other way—through the frequent doubling of characters, a device from popular literature and film, and for that matter, from fable and allegory, which ultimately allows him to develop theme.

In the primarily visual medium of film, the doubling of characters, often by emphasizing a surface physical resemblance, is a well-honed technique for suggesting psychological complexity and depth. Characters are often defined by who they come in contact with and, by implication, who they are *not*. The stressing of similarities between alter-egos has been used in films such as "The Searchers" (1956), "Psycho" (1960), or more recently "Schindler's List" (1993) to demonstrate the capacity for evil in essentially good characters, and vice versa.

Here, too, Faber is contrasted with his nemesis, Godliman, not only through the structural device of alternating chapters that parallel each other in length, word choice, and action—Faber kills in chapter 1; Godliman remembers killing in chapter 2;—but through similarities of background: both men live alone and have spent much of their time obsessed with a particular line of inquiry: Godliman's college thesis was even on a monk, sent on a clandestine mission, who was shipwrecked off the English coast—a fair description of what happens to Faber. Godliman becomes "wolfish" (71), a predator; Faber, the wolf in sheep's clothing, becomes "a good lover" (204), the "perfect man to have this with" (209), and for all intents and purposes, appears to be "a goodly man." But Faber is sullied because he is a professional spy; Godliman, in the classic linguistic shift favored by pre-war thriller writers, remains an "amateur" (132) and an agent of "Military Intelligence" (29).

Pre-war popular writers have also relied on an extensive use of the *dopplegaenger* technique to suggest split, or contrasting aspects of personality. Famous examples would include E. Phillips Oppenheim's *The Great Impersonation* (1920), Robert Louis Stevenson's *Dr. Jekyll and Mr. Hyde* (1886), or *The Master of Ballantrae* (1889), and, of course, Joseph Conrad's "The Heart of Darkness" (1902) and "The Secret Sharer" (1910)—two other works which also merge serious and popular forms.

In *Eye of the Needle,* Follett doubles Henry Faber with another character, David Rose, to show a different side of Henry's personality and to delineate him in clear contrast to the man he is not. Although Faber and David Rose, Lucy's crippled husband, are both described as emotionally repressed individuals on the run or wanting to run away (192), Faber is the ruthless killer of the future, machine-like and efficient, if dehumanized, while David remains rooted to an archaic schoolboy code of conduct regarding fair play (238) and heroism (273). In fact, Faber becomes a *replacement* for the anachronistic David Rose: he wears David's clothes, which fit; he uses David's razor and becomes the lover to his wife; in later scenes which parallel David's prior actions as an indifferent father, Faber "sat in silence, sipping coffee and listening to the rain and [the child's] voice" (277).

Several other pairings occur to increase our understanding of character and action. The one existing photograph of Faber, for example, is endlessly duplicated (154) and a number of false Fabers are arrested (178, 242), raising the question of his "true" identity, which Lucy will probe. As with a Graham Greene character, Faber is also pursued by a question of identity: throughout the novel, Faber has been afraid to look in mirrors (11); to see himself or who he is; it is the final pairing through a sexual liaison which will force an answer to this fundamental question.

Lucy's role, in fact, becomes increasingly central to the novel and toward the end one realizes that the trick of making the villain the hero cannot be sustained. Lucy, unbeknownst to the reader, has been the actual protagonist all along. By relying on a "suspense-fiction technique dating back to *Bleak House*," Follett bases "his taut scenario on seemingly unrelated plot lines," Josh Rubin has stated.[16] But the *relation* of the two plots, of course, is that one storyline has described Lucy's devil (Faber) and Lucy's angel (Godliman); the other, herself—a double focus which reaches past Dickens to Renaissance tragedy and medieval morality plays.

The allegorical elements in *Eye of the Needle* are clearest in the sections describing Lucy or anticipating her encounter with Faber. Early in the novel, she and David inhabit a kind of paradise from which they must fall. They are almost "too happy in their happiness." Shortly before David's car accident, he is described as being in perfect physical form, with "enormously long arms and legs" (24). Moments before the collision, Lucy, we are told, "felt very happy" (27). But it is a kind of fool's paradise they inhabit: on the surface, "[t]he whole thing [is] idyllic" (21) but their sexual transgression, their tasting of forbidden fruit, has led to "their first row" (26) and the "spice of guilt" (25).

Banished to an island, she and David must labor and suffer, emotionally and otherwise. In the same way that the fate of Dr. Faustus depends on his alliance with a good angel or a bad angel, the fate of

Lucy Rose will be decided by her siding with Faber (called "a devil" [102]), or with Professor Godliman, who later hovers over her through radio contact, and by her efforts to determine Faber's true identity.

In true allegorical fashion, Faber's progress toward the island is initially described as a *via dolorosa;* he feels a Christ-like stabbing pain in his side; he falls several times and gets to his knees to begin "the long, interminable crawl to [her] front door" (161). He has almost been impaled—crucified—on "a pointed rock like a stiletto sticking up . . . out of the wave" (160).

A handsome stranger, a false savior whom Lucy must first resurrect, he becomes a serpent in the garden, "a wolf in a sheepfold" (172). If this sexual predator has been made lame, Lucy's misdirected affection for him, her Mary Magdalene-like bathing of his wounds (250) is sufficient to renew desire—her own as well as Faber's.

It is through the sexual encounter itself, however, that true identity can be investigated and revealed. In an element from the category romance, the woman seeks to penetrate the man's personality, to peer beneath the mask and to sensitize him. In a long conversation in which they speculate on each other's lives, Faber is forced to "look away, into the fire" (192) and to answer the question of who he is, at least in terms of why he has never married. The individual who has been avoiding mirrors, doubles, and hiding his face the entire time must now look not only at himself but at his counterpart: at Lucy's own *via dolorosa* and unhappy marriage and at her symbolic shedding of blood (193).

Lucy's personal journey of discovery is likewise two-fold: she must find a "solution to [the] puzzle" (261) of Faber's personality and identity, and once she has realized that the good man in Faber "did not exist—she had imagined him" and that "instead of a warm, strong, affectionate man, she saw in front of her a monster" (267) she must then crush that reptile in the garden.

What is different about this contemporary re-telling of the myth of paradise lost and regained is that instead of two women—one who invites the serpent into the garden and the other who kills it—the modern woman is a self-actualizing composite of Eve and the Virgin Mary. Having "opened her eyes" (261) to his true nature, she blinds Faber temporarily "with a long-nailed forefinger" (279). Images of blindness or of averted sight occur throughout the novel, as do images of throbbing thumbs or fingers. In effect, Lucy seems unwilling to fully confront her own sexual duality, as hunter and hunted both. When Faber's "long-fingered hand" (292), phallic and serpentine, reaches in for her, she severs his two fingers but tears "her eyes away from the grotesque objects on the windowsill" (293).

But in order to save herself, or be fully integrated as a personality, she must confront what the severed objects on the windowsill symbolically represent—the more painful aspects of sexual penetration. With some advice from her "good angels," Lucy thrusts her own "three fingers into [a] live socket" (302) and transforms herself through this phallic insertion into a "mannish" (305) and admired hero, one capable of extreme action. The two sides of her own personality are fully fused: she can be both Eve, the sexual aggressor, and Mary, the virgin mother who will cause the serpent's "skull [to be] smashed like a glass goblet when [it] hit the rock" (304).

Follett's interests in popular psychology have been commented on by Andrew and Gina Macdonald writing for the *Dictionary of Literary Biography,* and Follett's admiration for strong women political leaders is well known.[17] Given his strict religious upbringing in the Plymouth Brethren, a reliance on Christian allegory is not surprising. In a probable swipe at the evangelical religion he had outgrown, Follett mentions a character in *Eye* whose "parents were both members of an obscure fundamentalist religious group" (180) and whose prescribed in-breeding had possibly resulted in the character being mentally deficient.

But religious allegory can also lead to symbol, as we have seen, and to theme, two largely defining elements of "serious" fiction. Interestingly, when discussing older forms of literature, especially literature which is largely allegorical, critics seldom make the distinction between "serious" and "popular." For example, how would one categorize the medieval morality play "Everyman," which has a serious didactic purpose but spoke to ordinary people, or for that matter, John Bunyan's *The Pilgrim's Progress* or the widely disseminated King James' version of *The Bible*? And Follett's purpose is, at times, didactic: drawing on archetypal as well as contemporary myth—the myth of the self-actualized woman who is capable of all deeds—he argues that admiration combined with affection is the key to love, and that war can bring out those qualities worth admiring.

War, with its promise of adventure and "heroism, full of color and people, millions of people" (264) can give the ordinary individual the motivation, the "inspiration" (280), to perform the extraordinary deed. Faber and Bloggs both admire Lucy, but if Lucy has "admired" Faber it is in wonder for an object she has not really understood, rather than from respect. Ultimately, the desire for external adventure is seen as a false desire: "Now, the desire for those things had left her, and she could not understand how she had ever wanted them" (293), a change paralleled by Bloggs' "older, harder, more cynical" (273) edge and Godliman's general war-weariness (295). Bloggs will replace the fatherly Godliman, first as a symbolic, then as an actual suitor, and Lucy's coming-of-age will be the recognition that the real adventure is the internal one, of "getting up in the morning and making breakfast . . . of cutting herbs from the garden and making pots of tea" (293), of living with someone whose admiration was mixed with affection (306).

In this sense and in others, the message of the melodrama—and of the allegory—is a conventional one: love conquers all and societal order will be restored. And yet *Eye of the Needle,* as MacLeish stated, "is a story that isn't ashamed to use all the traditional thriller devices of entertainment to serious ends—ideas about war, love, disappointment and hope."[18]

In his 1979 essay "Books That Enchant and Enlighten," written a few months after the publication of *Eye of the Needle,* Follett argued that both serious and popular fiction writers had "set themselves low standards." The elite "were allowed to dispense with plot, story, excitement, sensation, and the world outside the mind" while mass-market writers "were permitted cardboard characters, sloppy writing and [bland] texture."[19]

Concluding his essay, he urged fiction writers to aspire to something more, to the kind of blending of the serious and the popular such as Dickens, "the greatest novelist in the English language" (9), had achieved:

It is often said that a romance or a mystery can't be well characterized, true to life and beautifully written because everything has to be subordinate to plot. I think that's like saying verse will never have the impact of prose because the choice of words is constrained by metre and rhyme. In fact the rules of formal poetry give the words *more* impact. Plot ought to do the same for character. (29)

In *Eye of the Needle* Follett achieved this ideal.

5

CHANGE AND ADAPTATION IN *EYE OF THE NEEDLE*

The same year that Follett wrote his best-known and most successful espionage novel, *Eye of the Needle,* Bruce Merry published a critical study of the genre entitled *Anatomy of the Spy Thriller* (1977). In it, Merry maintains that the thrill in the thriller is often the result of formal techniques, most notably, structure. Merry, in fact, graphs Frederick Forsyth's *The Day of the Jackal* to reveal a rigid funneling technique that "packs more and more action and information into less and less space," obliging the reader to "accelerate his speed of consumption."[1]

During his tenure at Everest Books, Follett had come to realize that much could be learned from studying other people's works. "For construction, we'll emulate *The Day of the Jackal* rather than *Nicholas Nickleby,*"[2] he has said in arguing for quality popular fiction. But if the classic plot structure of *The Day of the Jackal* was apparent to those like Follett who admired it, Follett's own use of a telescoping plot in *Eye of the Needle* has been less obvious. He admitted as much in a 1987 introduction to a re-issued work:

Eye of the Needle has an even more rigid structure [than his earlier works] although nobody to my knowledge has ever noticed it: there are six parts, each with six chapters (except for the last part, which has seven), the first chapter in each part dealing with the spy, the second with the spy catchers, and so on until the sixth, which always tells of the international military consequences of what has gone before. (*PM* vi)

The Day of the Jackal and *Eye of the Needle,* two examples of the successful use of a telescoping plot, have often been compared. Not only did Follett admire the Forsyth novel and read it "to see why it sold so many copies,"[3] but both books are in the tradition of such "manhunt" thrillers as Household's *Rogue Male* or Richard Condon's *The Manchurian Candidate* (1959). In addition to sharing similar plot patterns and subject matter, *The Day of the Jackal* and *Eye of the Needle* were also considered "first novels" that enjoyed a popular international reception. Within three years, *The Day of the Jackal* had sold 6 million copies; through careful marketing, *Eye of the Needle* achieved similar sales within an even shorter time, moving onto the bestseller lists weeks before actual publication and initially selling 5 million copies worldwide.[4] In reality, of course, Frederick Forsyth and Ken Follett had both been writing and publishing novels for years, but these two carefully constructed chase melodramas represented an international success, and both novels were soon turned into films.

Here the similarities cease: "The Day of the Jackal" was one of the top grossing films of 1973 and has been hailed as "a suspense classic [that] is put together like a fine watch." Throughout the 1970s, the movie remained one of the most popular political thrillers, with most critics agreeing that it was a deft re-creation of the book, one that "managed to keep all the heart-pounding thrills of the novel intact."[5]

The film version "Eye of the Needle," on the other hand, placed a "disappointing fifty-fifth on *Variety*'s list of 'Big Rental Films'" and took in only $6,661,265 at the box office. When released in 1981, the movie received mixed to negative reviews, with David Ansen of *Newsweek* observing that "'Eye of the Needle' never really catches fire . . . and was a better movie as a book."[6]

What becomes apparent, then, is that simply following a ready-made plot structure does not always guarantee a production team an equally successful film, as the two examples should illustrate. This disparity between the original material and later interpretations raises important questions about the adaptation process itself, the fundamental differences between fiction and film (even within popular genres), and the artistic integrity of a source novel.

André Bazin has pointed out that "[t]he more important and decisive the literary qualities of the work, the more the adaptation disturbs its equilibrium, the more it needs a creative talent to reconstruct it on a new equilibrium."[7] Novels with a particular verbal texture, a considerable use of memory, thought, introspection and subjective distortions of time are, of course, the novels which are most difficult to transfer to the screen— at least in a fashion that remains recognizably close to the original. On the other hand, books which show little interest in the art of the novel and are primarily plot-driven may be the easiest to adapt.

Forsyth's novel may have been less discursive than presentational. His style has been described as visual rather than emotive and "a model of clarity and simplicity . . . that allows the reader a *view* of plot and character apparently untrammeled by authorial guidance" (emphasis added). When turned into a film, "The Day of the Jackal" was considered a faithful adaptation of "Forsyth's best seller, registering frame by frame, as is director Zinnemann's style, a precise, almost painful reconstruction of the story,"[8] thus preserving the strict funneling effect of the novel.

Follett's book, in contrast, was praised both for its intricacy of plot and its writing quality. In his book review for the *Washington Post,* Roderick MacLeish argued that Follett brings the villain "slowly to life, developing and complicating him with a skillful leisure"—a leisure which is perhaps antithetical to the demands of the film thriller. Follett lamented the cinematic liberties taken with his own ending and cursed "the producers of the thing. In the book, [the evil spy] falls off a cliff; that wasn't dramatic enough for the movies, I gather, so they wrote their own version."[9]

The process of adaptation, of course, ultimately alters the original to some extent and becomes an interpretation of it. In his classic study *Novels into Film* (1957), George Bluestone pointed out that "[w]e discover . . . in film versions of the novel, an inevitable abandonment of 'novelistic' elements."[10] What we will find in the following pages, through a discussion of the differences between the book and the movie version of *Eye of the Needle,* is that certain inherent strengths of the novel remained untranslated, that the filmmakers only on occasion found cinematic equivalents for those strengths, and that despite the relative weakness of the film version, the adaptation still provides useful insights into the novel.

When writing *Eye of the Needle* in 1977, Follett may well have understood the principal differences between novels and films. As we have seen, Follett's literary models were alternately popular and serious, but were textual nonetheless. In an essay written shortly after the publication of *Eye of the Needle,* he reflected on the importance of writing books that would have "the merits of pulp fiction" as well as the "virtues we expect of serious fiction,"[11] and this interest ended in a blending of romantic storyline and literary texture that was difficult to retain in the film.

For the most part, the stylistic strengths of *Eye of the Needle* are the result of what contemporary literature does best—experiment with point-of-view and internalize external event, as the following passage makes clear:

She sipped her drink and considered whether she ought to make the first move. Mr. Faber was obviously shy—chronically shy. He wasn't sexless—she could tell by the look in his eyes on the two occasions he had seen her in her nightdress. Perhaps she could overcome his shyness by being brazen. What did she have to lose? She tried imagining the worst, just to see what it felt like. Suppose he rejected her. Well, it would be embarrassing—even humiliating. It would be a blow to her pride. But nobody else need know it had happened. He would just have to leave. (7)

An obvious difference between fiction and film is the ability of contemporary literature to enter the subconscious, to explore the psychology of a character from the inside looking out. We find in the above passage the well-established literary technique for the rendering of thought on the printed page: the use of questions, the dialogue with the self giving the sense of inquiry and discovery, and language or expression matched to a particular character, thus bringing the minor character of the landlady to life and humanizing her through her sexual frustration and her hesitation.

If we compare this moment in the story with the same scene in the film—the moment at which the widowed landlady decides to barge in on Faber (the spy) and is therefore killed by him—we notice that the film-makers have not communicated internal motivation as effectively. In the film, the landlady is portrayed as having a mild, possibly only motherly concern for Faber. Although she is shown holding a red rose—a visual indicator for romance—her primary concern seems to be the meal she is cooking for him. Shown only from the outside, her real reason for intruding can only be guessed at, and most viewers would probably readily accept her surface excuse that she is just bringing him his food. What is lost, therefore, what has not been captured in this visual treatment, is the note of irony ("What did she have to lose?") which deftly characterizes the landlady as both lonely and self-deceived.

In part, the early 20th-century literary shift away from the meticulous description of external reality in favor of a more internalized consciousness can be explained as a retreat from the competition of motion pictures. The strength of film is in showing and de-*pict*-ing, in creating a verisimilitude with much greater economy and immediacy than literature can hope to achieve. For example, in the film version of "Eye of the Needle," a series of traveling helicopter shots above an actual Scottish island, the Isle of Mull, effectively establishes the size, the shape and the bleakness of the locale in a mere 25 seconds. The novel, on the other hand, requires 13 full paragraphs to "show" the reader the island.

What the novel can less obtrusively offer, however, is a verbal interpretation of the island through diction and tone, the authorial guidance that some critics have found noticeably lacking in Forsyth's writing. Establishing the island, Follett writes: "Around most of its coast the cliffs rise out of the cold sea without the courtesy of a beach. Angered by this rudeness the waves pound on the rocks with impotent rage; a ten-thousand year fit of bad temper that the island ignores with impunity" (37). The novelist's impression is communicated, of course, through the selection of certain connotative words—"rudeness," "impotent," and "impunity"—as well as the devices of personification and hyperbole. In addition to the lyrical quality of the writing created by these devices, a shaping or control of language takes place as well. The reader is not only shown, but also told how to see a particular stretch of terrain. If a similar shaping takes place through the high angle shot of the island, it is both more economical as well as less forceful.

Other writing qualities which are generally associated with a literary rather than a mass-market approach would be an interest in language for its own sake, an emphasis on character rather than on plot, and a use of metaphor and simile which may or may not become symbolic. In certain passages in Follett's *Eye of the Needle,* the prose style becomes Biblical, as in the following:

So she did not cry, and she did not drink the brandy, and she did not leave the island; but instead she went upstairs and got into bed, and lay awake beside her sleeping husband, listening to the wind and trying not to think, until the gulls began to call, and a grey rainy dawn crept over the North Sea and filled the little bedroom with a cold, pale light, and at last she went to sleep. (47)

In other sections, the writing makes use of the authoritative tones of an early 20th-century omniscient narrator—a particularly useful technique for interweaving multiple plot strands and the vast amounts of background information found in many spy novels:

Driving through England in the blackout was a weird experience. One missed lights that one hadn't realized were there before the war: lights in cottage porches and farmhouse windows, lights on cathedral spires and inn signs, and—most of all—the luminous glow, low in the distant sky, of the thousand lights of a nearby town. (27)

The above passage seems more indebted to E. M. Forster, and the knowledgeable voice of the travelogue writer or the historian, than it does to Frederick Forsyth and his pared-down journalistic prose.

Film has never been particularly adept at rendering mental states—memory, dream, imagination—or the interpretation of reality through metaphor. Attempts at showing inner life by means other than an actor's facial expression or gesture, techniques such as voice-over, dream sequences or flashbacks, have generally been considered less-than-satisfactory equivalents for what frequently takes place in novels. Follett's novel contains numerous sections detailing memory, dreams or fears, as well as figurative descriptions ("he had to detour around a lake, its surface a silver mirror under the moon" [102], or "Lying on its side, the jeep looked powerful but helpless, like a wounded elephant" [268]), which add a poetic, almost symbolic, quality. More importantly, as we have noted, metaphor is also an attribute of thought. The jeep, in the above example, looks powerful and helpless to *someone*—and all of these techniques add internal resonance and characterization for which a film must find some compensatory approach.

So what are some of the advantages that film holds over fiction and how are these advantages put to use in the movie adaptation "Eye of the Needle"?

In the first place, as we have seen, an economical depiction of concrete reality is a primary advantage film holds over fiction. Second, editing—the combination of shots to create intellectual associations or comparisons for the viewer—can sometimes be used artistically as an equivalent for literary metaphor. In the filmed sequence in which Faber sets out in a stolen boat, for example, close ups of a radio dial, a spinning compass, a ring, a watch, a bulb—all round things—are intercut with other circular objects: the moon disappearing behind a cloud, fuel gauges, the hollow of the cove, a life preserver, rings of ocean foam, the actor's eyes themselves. Combined with tight framing and set design, the impression is one of entrapment, and the images of circularity reinforce the idea that Faber can never really escape.

In the third place, the ability of film to record actual motion, movement, or action is also a strength. Fiction, of course, can only state that movement occurred, and while film also gives us the illusion of motion, it comes closer to the primary experience. In the film version of "Eye of the Needle," during one of the numerous escapes that are part of the genre, Faber steals a motorcycle instead of the Morris motorcar described in the book: the actor, Donald Sutherland, is now completely unenclosed. Temporary freedom is also suggested through a combination of traveling shots, point-of-view shots, and, most importantly, left to right movement across the frame, indicating rapid progression.

Last, an actor's dramatic interpretation through voice, facial expression, emotion, and gesture may sometimes be an equivalent for characterization in a novel. In a review of the movie "Eye of the Needle," Janet Maslin of the *New York Times* opined that "[a]ll of the film's important touches come from within its characters" as when Donald Sutherland abandons the stolen motorcycle, then "turns around and straightens out his suit with a briskness that speaks volumes about Faber's eerie resourcefulness."[12]

In these examples, the filmmakers are using the true resources of the cinema rather than attempting to recreate the exact effects of the book. In the words of the pioneer film critic Rudolf Arnheim each art form "reaches the heights in its own way,"[13] and where the filmmakers are most conscious of their cinematic antecedents, rather than considerate of the source novel, and where they have creatively exploited the unique elements of their medium—sound, camerawork, acting, set design, and editing—is where "Eye of the Needle" contains its most engaging moments.

We have already considered what was lost in the translation of the section in which the prying landlady is murdered: but what the filmmakers bring to this same section, in addition to more physical confrontation through the staging and a sense of foreboding through the use of low angles, tight framing, and subjective camera shots, is the creative use of sound—in this case, music—to create self-referencing and a recognition of genre. By playing a facetious music hall song on the radio ("Oh, it's just a casual meeting/Dare I give your hand a squeeze?/For your little Pomeranian/Has seen my little Pekinese"), the filmmakers use situational irony to effectively comment on the violent action, and allude to a similar incongruous use of music in crime films ranging from Fritz Lang's "M" (1931) to Orson Welles' "Touch of Evil" (1958).

The score itself is an acknowledgment of classics within the genre. Written by Miklos Rozsa, who scored "Spellbound" (1945) and "A Double Life" (1947), it was termed a "particularly stylish" romantic evocation of the era, and includes numerous musical allusions to other Rozsa scores such as "Double Indemnity" (1944) and "The Killers" (1964). In the same way, the lighting, set design and camerawork contain, at times, deliberate references to earlier films: when Donald Sutherland stands half in shadow beneath a street lamp, the viewer might be watching "The Spy in Black" (1939). When he rushes up the stairs to his transmitter hidden in a London flat, it might be the staircase scene in "The Man Who Never Was" (1955). And when he crosses the cottage sitting room, sinisterly lit through an old cucaloris, it might be any of a dozen *films noir* with their shifting shadows on the wall and their high contrast, low key lighting. These touches of Fritz Lang, Billy Wilder, and Anatole Litvak were considered "reminiscent tidbits" which "only enhance[d] the overall production."[14]

But it probably is not possible to make a spy melodrama set in England in the 1940s without giving some thought to the style and *mise en scène* of Alfred Hitchcock's works. Such a tribute "Eye of the Needle" clearly makes, especially in the railroad carriage scenes where one thinks of "The Lady Vanishes" (1938) or "Strangers on a Train" (1951), and in the escape across the railroad trestles and the moors, which seems indebted to "The Thirty-Nine Steps" (1935). If "Eye of the Needle" remains uneven as a film, it is perhaps because the production team lose sight of their actual cinematic antecedents—the compression and frenetic pacing of an Alfred Hitchcock film—and instead grasp for the subtext of emotion in an attempt to stay "faithful" to original literary material.

In consequence, where the film "Eye of the Needle" becomes less-than-satisfactory is where it fails to capitalize on the strengths of cinema and instead looks to certain qualities of the novel—in particular, the complexity of plot, the gradations of character, and the subtext of emotion.

In dissecting the plot structure of the spy novel, Bruce Merry pointed out that "the important feature common to all spy narratives" is the use of multiple storylines, of "significant events occurring simultaneously at different parts of the globe."[15] In the same way that a vast panorama of settings and characters was an important part of the 19th-century novel and *required* an all-knowing, ironic, authoritative narrator, so too this particular device is resurrected in the post-war espionage novel in order to achieve a similar effect: the integration and resolution of seemingly separate storylines. To achieve this, Follett, in his mature work, has almost always relied on an omniscient point-of-view.

Filmmakers, when faced with the vast tableau of the traditional novel and its all-seeing point-of-view, have sometimes reduced multiple plot strands to a single thread: the 1954 version of Steinbeck's *East of Eden* is an example. On the other hand, in order to retain "the most important feature" of the spy thriller, many filmmakers will attempt to include a hint of the various plot lines. This delicate balance between the demands of the genre, as it has come down to us in popular novels, and the demands of film, especially in terms of audience viewing time, is not always readily achievable. Fred Zinnemann, who adapted Frederick Forsyth's *Day of the Jackal,* may have erred in one direction: a film historian has called the plot "impossibly complex, plagued by hundreds of loose ends that made no sense until the climax." Richard Marquand, who staged "Eye of the Needle," may have erred in the opposite direction: in the film, not only is the romantic story resolution missing (in which the lonely detective Bloggs falls in love with the heroine, Lucy, in a Dickensian interweaving of all story threads), but a key character—Professor Godliman, the spycatcher—remains, in the view of David Ansen, an "undeveloped role" that wasted the talents of the actor, Ian Bannen.[16]

Other criticisms of the film were also largely related to plot structure. Janet Maslin, in her arts section review, seemed to feel that the movie's scenes were separate units rather than coherent parts of a seamless plot: "[T]he central portion," she argued, "is by far the most successful . . . [and] becomes something from which the film never recovers," while Rob Edelman, in a survey of 1981 films, stated that "[t]he first section of the film is rather difficult to follow because of its seemingly unrelated parallel action."[17]

Problems in the handling of competing plot lines are also related to problems in developing the characterization of Faber and Lucy. In the novel, written with "a skillful leisure," character change can be shown over many sections—and well before the climax of the story. We have already seen what was gained in the film by having Faber steal a motorcycle instead of a car. In the novel, however, the theft of the car allows for an encounter with two charming, elderly women, and thus the gradual sensitizing of the villain: when he abandons the broken vehicle, he "felt a twinge of regret for Emma and Jessie, who would find it very difficult to get their car repaired before the end of the war" (151). In essence, these various encounters humanize Faber and allow us to believe in his vulnerability long before he actually meets Lucy on the island.

The rapidly accelerating pace and increased speed of consumption that Merry considered hallmarks of the spy thriller are further obscured by the film's late development of motivation. By having much of the characterization take place early in the novel, Follett could focus on action toward the end. In the film, by contrast, Faber's humanity is presented for the first time quite late in the story. In addition, this presentation is made through external actions alone—dialogue and gesture —rather than through a combination of those actions with internal responses—thought and reflection—as it had been managed in the book. In the movie version, the two actors (Donald Sutherland and Kate Nelligan) are restricted to speaking their thoughts out loud in a series of static discussions—in the sitting room, on the cliffs, walking along the beach, in the cave—that ends up halting the forward progression called for in the genre.

This weakness resulting from the need to express emotional subtext is particularly conspicuous toward the end. Well after the technical climax of the film, a new scene and new dialogue were included to show how the characters feel: "The war's come down to the two of us," Donald Sutherland tries to say with some conviction. "I did what I had to do." Film critic David Ansen as well as cinema historian Rob Edelman both called attention to these especially trite lines.

Emotional turmoil and character change can, of course, be effectively and subtly conveyed in the movies: Luchino Visconti's adaptation of "Death in Venice" (1971) substituted evocative music and an actor's diffident glances for the novel's introspection—but that technique was used throughout the film.

When a similar technique is used in "Eye of the Needle," the audience is largely unprepared for it: instead of the book's quick ending (where Faber is killed and the story moves almost directly to an epilogue), the two principal actors must suddenly emote, staring at each other endlessly with long, lingering, anxiety-ridden gazes because the character Lucy must shoot her former lover. The romantic cliché is extended as the music predictably swells to greater and greater heights, until Lucy finally runs out of bullets. Although the structural demands of the spy thriller would suggest that the film should rush to its conclusion, the necessity of externalizing character change had won out. Follett's own assessment of the structurally flawed ending was that the evil spy "takes fifteen minutes to bloody die. By that time the audience is roaring with laughter, and if they start laughing in a melodrama, you've had it."[18]

Although the director, Richard Marquand, went on to make "Return of the Jedi" (1983), "Until September" (1984), and "Jagged Edge" (1985), his experience at that time was largely in British television. The casting of Kate Nelligan, who was then appearing on "Masterpiece Theater," as well as the use of frequent close-ups and low contrast ratios, gave the movie the appearance of a television production. One can only speculate on the outcome had a more experienced and innovative director made the film. As reviewer Janet Maslin put it, "Alfred Hitchcock could have worked miracles with this story's mixture of love, suspicion and intrigue,"[19] and it is interesting to consider the changes Alfred Hitchcock *did* make with Buchan's *The Thirty-Nine Steps* (1915), from adding-in a love element to creating the famous music hall scene to changing the meaning of the 39 steps itself (from a literal beach stairway to the name of a clandestine organization), all in the name of simplification and cohesion. In part, reduction is necessary because of the difference between viewing time and reading time. The consumer of a novel can re-read passages, contemplate them, skip forward or back, and imaginatively envision scenes; the viewer of a film can only see or hear a moment once.

To even argue whether or not a film is faithful to the original is, in the view of some critics, "aesthetically irresponsible"[20] since the significance of a work derives from the fresh, creative treatment of source material, from the imaginative transmutation of it as a source into something which exists in and of itself as film.

In its moments of cinematic homage, the film "Eye of the Needle" meets those ends and also offers an important insight into the novel, demonstrating that Follett's book is both nostalgic and formulaic; and where the film becomes muddled, it acknowledges the special qualities of the novel, its literary flavor and language.

"Day of the Jackal" may have been the more successful film, in part because of the timeliness of its assassination topic, but Frederick Forsyth's prose style in his novel has little to recommend it besides narrative efficiency. Writing, in his case, means plot construction and reported information. To suggest, therefore, that "The Day of the Jackal" is a better film because it is closer to the original may be less an indication of the novel's literary worth than a criticism of it.

6

TELEVISION AS INTERPRETATION:
THE KEY TO REBECCA

As early in the history of film criticism as 1932, Rudolf Arnheim recognized in his study *Film As Art* that great literature does not necessarily result in great films and that in fact the converse may be true; that mediocre novels generally make the most interesting films. Taking this idea a step further, some commentators would maintain that if a work of art has already achieved its fullest artistic expression in one medium, the transference into another medium will inevitably fail—a view popularly expressed by John Simon who has categorically stated that "*always* either the book or the film is less than absolutely first rate.*" While this would be an extreme view, one that would hold that no adaptation of *Catcher in the Rye* could equal the original, such classics of the cinema as "Strangers on a Train" and "Psycho" would seem to support Alfred Hitchcock's own observation that most attempts to film a classic novel "probably wouldn't be any good."[1]

As we have seen, Arnheim maintained that each medium reaches artistic heights in its own way. "If we call literature the most complete medium of all," he argued, "we have to remember, nevertheless, that this universality also makes for weaknesses, where other media show particular strength."[2] So too, in Arnheim's view, film must capitalize on its own limitations: if the absence of sound, the absence of color and the lack of three-dimensional depth have since been addressed by technical innovation (to the detriment of the artistry of film, according to Arnheim), some noteworthy differences between fiction and film remain and must be exploited for the benefit of each medium.

In more recent years, the television mini-series has become a principal means for the adaptation of novels. Only one of Follett's novels, *Eye of the Needle,* was turned into a theatrically released film: three other books, *The Key to Rebecca, Lie Down with Lions* and *The Third Twin,* have been adapted as television movies, and while the television movie uses many of the resources of film, it must also capitalize on its own intrinsic limitations in size, scope and budget. In this chapter, we will discuss Follett's relationship to film and television, and the adaptive/ interpretive process as it has been applied to his novels.

We have noted already that Follett's literary apprenticeship included the novelization of an existing film script. Much has been written on the impact of literature on film, but a reverse influence is also worth considering—ways in which popular film and television have created change in the novel. The most obvious influences would probably be in an increasing reliance on dialogue; the use of chapter "hooks" and the intercutting of scenes; as well as narrative patterns that rely on action, surprise and plot twists. Follett's novels have been termed "cinematic in conception" and are often written from a strict outline. Increasingly, he has moved from the "graceful, powerful prose" and careful "character development" he once admonished popular writers to strive for,[3] toward a more direct expository narrative style and a greater use of dialogue.

"I read [thrillers] for professional reasons," he noted a few years later, "to find out what my competitors are up to," and when one considers the simplified writing style of Robert Ludlum, Jack Higgins—or, in this country, John Grisham and Tom Clancy, whose works have frequently been turned into film—it is not surprising that in the interest of remaining a viable popular writer, Follett's novels have sometimes shown the influence of cinema, even if that influence has come indirectly, through the reading of his sales rivals. In 1989, he stated that "[t]he distinguishing characteristic of entertainment fiction, which is what I write, is that the story is paramount. To that end, the characters are custom-made to fit the plot,"[4] a description that could as readily be applied to most television and film.

His own direct involvement in the cinematic arts has been infrequent and somewhat ambiguous. In interviews, he seldom mentions film and his stated models are almost entirely literary. "I compare myself to the great classical writers," he has said. "Why compare myself to John le Carré when you might just as well compare yourself to, say, Jane Austen? I compare myself all the time with great English writers like Dickens and Thomas Hardy and George Eliot—and wonder why I can't do better."[5] And yet, after the publication success of *Eye of the Needle*, Follett wrote two television scripts for the BBC, "Fringe Banking" (1978) and "A Football Star" (1979), and also developed a film treatment for *The Key to Rebecca* and a script for *Lie Down with Lions*. When those two novels were turned into television movies a few years later, however, the scripts were by other writers—Samuel Harris for "The Key to Rebecca," and the team of Guy Andrews and Julian Bond for "Lie Down with Lions." *Triple* was optioned but never produced.[6] "The Third Twin" was broadcast as a television movie in 1997, with a script by Cindy Myers.

A production team may exert a clarifying and heightening interpretation on a novel or may produce a film which not only fails to thoroughly capitalize on the true strengths of cinema or television, but which may also lose sight of the essence of the source novel. In the view of one television critic, for example, the production "The Key to Rebecca" (1985) effectively "transformed [Follett's novel] into a sweeping World War II story of intrigue and betrayal[;] The photography is lush, the sets authentic." By contrast, the script for "Lie Down with Lions" (1994) was called "stupefying [and] by-the-numbers," and the story a "melodrama . . . stretched to absurdity [that] has little to do with the Follett novel."[7]

A comparison of Follett's *The Key to Rebecca* with the production based on it, as well as some reference to the book and the film of *The Third Twin,* will demonstrate that whenever a work of fiction is turned into a television movie, it is transformed by various means: the tools of film (camera, editing, performance, set design, music and cinematic conventions); the writer's and director's particular vision and ideology, and the selection and reduction process fundamental to a presentational art form. In these two instances—the adaptation of Follett's *The Key to Rebecca* and *The Third Twin*—the transformation process itself may have exerted a useful restraint, solidifying the plotline and purpose in the first instance and tempering the explicit ideology in the second.

"I suppose," Follett reflected in a 1980 interview, "that I'm continually looking over my shoulder and wondering if what I'm doing is as good as *Eye of the Needle*." At the time of the interview, he was promoting a new espionage thriller, *The Key to Rebecca,* which, as a main selection of the Book-of-the-Month Club, an initial printing of 100,000 copies, and serialization in several magazines was already assured bestselling status in advance of the reviews.[8]

Although Follett had spent an entire year writing the novel—a considerably longer time than he had expended on his two previous novels, *Eye of the Needle* and *Triple*[9]—this time the careful crafting of material did not result in an always flawless interweaving of historical information, character, and genre. Several critics concluded that *The Key to Rebecca* was a pale imitation of *Eye of the Needle,* that the two books shared a similar World War II backdrop, a keen attention to historical detail and the inclusion of a sympathetic female point-of-view, but that in general *The Key to Rebecca* was decidedly second-rate.

Reviewer Robert Lekachman, for example, termed the novel "rather tame;" Peter Andrews, in an unremittingly negative critique, called it "mechanical" and "dreary;" and Frederick Busch, of the *Chicago Tribune,* noted that toward the end, the novel descends into an embarrassing and unnecessary interior monologue.[10] If Follett's ability to blend popular and serious forms had made *Eye of the Needle* a praiseworthy contribution to the thriller form, that smooth merging of patterns and types had not quite occurred in his 1980 book.

Even in a favorable review written by Joseph McLellan for the *Washington Post Book World,* there is the implication that *The Key to Rebecca* straddles two literary approaches: "It is a novel primarily in the post-Helen MacInnes school, rather than the post-Ian Fleming school. . . . Its characters and action are, on the whole, slower-moving, less chrome-hard and glittery, not quite so eccentric or one-dimensional,"[11] all of which might suggest that the story, when turned into a television film, could actually benefit from the inevitable process of distillation and condensation.

The central weakness in *The Key to Rebecca* is perhaps that of obviousness. Set in the Egyptian desert on the eve of the battle for Tobruk, it details the efforts of a German-Arab spy, Wolff, to penetrate behind British lines and gain access to Allied defense plans. Using Du Maurier's *Rebecca* to create a code, he transmits messages back to Rommel until tracked down by a British officer, Major Vandam.

If the plotline seems overly familiar, it is no doubt because the book code device has appeared in many spy novels, as has the "behind the enemy lines on the eve of a battle" motif. The story, including the love affair with a Cairo belly dancer, was based largely on the true-life account of Nazi spy John Eppler, and a non-fiction book on this subject had appeared in 1958. (The Eppler story has been used again as recently as 1992 in Michael Ondaatje's *The English Patient.*)

Positive reviews of *The Key to Rebecca* tended to praise the use of historical detail, the slower moving characterization, the descriptions of Cairo during World War II and the wealth of information about the desert, nomadic life, the rise of Egyptian Nationalism, and the progress of the battle for Tobruk—in other words, the *combination* of fiction and non-fiction writing. However, the very fact that the component parts become so noticeable might suggest a kind of synthetic quality to the book.

Instead of personal history being fully a part of a character's thoughts, for example, it often appears as a short, biographical entry: "She had been the eldest of five children in a desperately poor family. Her parents were cultured and loving people. . . . When Elene was fifteen years old her father began to go blind," etc.[12]

Descriptive passages for local flavor also seem systematic and devoid of authorial guidance: "There were countless uniforms—not just British but Australian, New Zealand, Polish, Yugoslav, Palestinian, Indian and Greek" (31). Or from the following page: "There were a dozen or so well-known pensions catering for tourists of different nationalities: Swiss, Austrian, German, Danish and French" (32). Some writers, such as Saul Bellow, use the technique of the catalogue to suggest texture and thought, but the listing is usually linked to an ironic interpretation; without such, it becomes a kind of obligatory detailing.

This quality of the dutiful inclusion of information is even more apparent in other sections that require a strong point-of-view. A young Anwar Sadat enters the novel and thinks to himself: "Six months later Sadat had suffered another failure. This time it centered on Egypt's fat, licentious, Turkish King. The British gave an ultimatum to King Farouk," etc. (73).

Years later, after having written several other books which incorporated history, Follett stated that "the skill of creating suspense in a non-fiction book lies in the arrangement of the material, such as choosing from whose point of view to tell a particular scene, [and] finding ways to make the kind of tedious, everyday situations that go into a real-life story more gripping."[13] We have seen how point-of-view and irony created intimacy with characters in *Eye of the Needle*. In the above section on Sadat's background, a distancing effect is created instead by having Sadat recall the central events of his political life in the style of a non-fiction article, a technique which is also used for other important characters, resulting in similar dispensable blocks of information: "Vandam's wartime career had so far been distinguished by one spectacular success and one great failure. The failure took place in Turkey" (22), and the two-part paragraph will predictably shift to Vandam's major success, prompting one to agree with Virginia Woolf's assessment of traditional fiction that nobody really thinks that way.

If the Joycean interior monologue moves us closer to how the mind at rest actually functions, when such a technique is included in *The Key to Rebecca* it seems incompatible with the drive and thrust of an espionage thriller and reads instead as *A Portrait of Anwar Sadat as a Young Boy*—"I am a small boy. My father told me how old I am, but I forgot. I will ask him again next time he comes home. . . . I go to school. I learn the Koran. The Koran is a holy book" (70). Perhaps Follett never quite found the right locus for this novel; the point-of-view is alternately too close to the character, or too distant.

Unlike *Eye of the Needle,* which fused serious and popular concerns, *The Key to Rebecca* shifts awkwardly between the high literary and the mass-market. When the Modernist interior monologue is used again a mere forty pages before the end of the novel—at a juncture where a thriller necessitates closure—it seems, at the very least, extrinsic to the genre. Having finished with this brief paean to Modernism, it's back to the exigencies of plot. As noted by reviewer Frederick Busch, these include a fist-fight, a "'High Noon" rescue of the wounded hero by his gal . . . a miraculous rainstorm in the desert, a last page blooming of flowers in barrenness, and a long kiss held until the lights come up"[14]—references, of course, to cinematic rather than novelistic devices. Ultimately, it is the attempt in the text to combine disparate elements that results in both hesitancy and misdirection.

In the previous chapter, we observed that the stylistic strengths of *Eye of the Needle* worked to a certain extent against its filmic treatment. "The danger with . . . adaptations," the screenwriter and director of *Emma* has noted, "particularly of English novels, is that, as the screenwriter, if you love the language, you want to keep as much of it as possible."[15] Given the need for some revision in *The Key to Rebecca,* the production team for the television movie was perhaps less reverential. In essence, it may be reasonable to suggest that the adaptation process itself, which requires that scenes be cut, minor characters simplified or eliminated, and subplots dispensed with, imposed a necessary tightening on a novel unsure of itself.

There are various ways in which this strengthening took place:

First, as we have noted before, film adaptations, and by implication, made-for-television films, are uniquely suited to deal with external reality and to render through image and sound what often requires several pages to describe. In the movie "The Key to Rebecca," a single establishing shot in the bazaar, with its blur of soldiers hurrying past and its film extras of many different races, the noise of car horns and vendors on the soundtrack, the call of the *muezzin,* and the right-to-left screen movement suggestive of commotion, creates the requisite atmosphere within a few brief seconds. Without either the lyrical quality or ironic tone of authorial guidance used for similar place descriptions in *Eye of the Needle,* the many pages of travelogue in *The Key to Rebecca* become static and informational—qualities avoided in the film through the well-established technique of combining moving horizontal lines—the marching soldiers—with strong verticals—the columns in the bazaar and the key character, Elene, who moves downscreen.

Second, we have also discussed ways in which editing can be a substitute for figurative language. In the film, swift intercutting between the German spy, played by David Soul, and the spycatcher, played by Cliff Robertson, suggests a connection between the two men within the first few minutes of the film. Because of the novel's tentative steps in various directions (the story of a man's failure, his relationship with his son, the story of the Egyptian campaign generally), this fundamental doubling of the hunter and the hunted does not become apparent until much later in the novel and is created largely through the contrasting love interests—Vandam becomes involved with the Jewish nationalist, Elene; Wolff exploits the Egyptian belly dancer, Sonja. The use of film editing is therefore both more economical and, in this instance, more symbolic.

Third, we can again argue that an awareness of literary or filmic antecedents is important to popular forms. If the novel *The Key to Rebecca* seems uncertain of its origins and its direction—is it to be a Modernist exploration of consciousness, a popular *dopplegaenger* tale, or the gothic romance suggested by the title?—the made-for-television movie seems more clearly and consistently rooted in cinematic and television history. From the music reminiscent of "Lawrence of Arabia" (1962) and "Raiders of the Lost Ark" (1981) to a bathtub murder scene recalling the subjective camerawork and the suggestive editing in "Psycho" (1960) and "Sabotage" (1936), the filmmakers seem cognizant of distinct film codes and conventions. Such tropes, in fact, find their real origin in the expressive art of the silent film, and it is interesting to note how many of the strongest moments in the movie—the chase down the alleyway, the search through the German spy's house, even Cliff Robertson's longing for his dead wife—are expressed non-verbally.

The search through the German spy's house exemplifies the tightening and heightening process that takes place when filmmakers impose a visual and aural logic on a scene which had been described verbally. In the novel *The Key to Rebecca,* the spycatcher decides to break into Wolff's Cairo residence and investigate. While the *process* of investigation is detailed, and the factual and informational quality of the writing lends a certain credibility to the scene, little seems at stake since neither the spy nor the spycatcher is in danger. A simple shift in the film, however, places the German spy in the house and in a particularly vulnerable position—asleep in his bed. When the spycatcher enters, the German spy hides and it is now Cliff Robertson who is vulnerable—with his back to the camera in most shots. The search takes place without a word being spoken but the classic elements of movie suspense—high contrast lighting, the intercutting between close-ups of the hunter and the hunted, the noise of the wind and of footsteps, and suitably eerie violin and oboe music turn what had been a relatively flat, expository scene into film melodrama.

The production team's willingness to fully exploit an interior location also places "Eye of the Needle" firmly within television traditions. As Howard Newcombe has pointed out in "Towards a Television Aesthetic," the smallness of the screen, the limitations of budget, and the restrictions of studio shooting often make television drama the art of the indoors rather than the outdoors. Rooms define the background, aspirations, and social status of characters, and the frequent use of enclosed space creates an intimacy and focus on personal problems.[16]

This is certainly the case with the television adaptation of *The Key to Rebecca*. The imperialist attitude of Wolff is conveyed through the interior set design: the high ceiling and white walls of his home are overtly colonial. So too, the hard-working, pragmatic Vandam is defined by his office decor, which is government-functional, modest and in creative disarray. Most scenes of character development take place within rooms: Vandam with his son in the sitting room; Wolff and Sonja inside the houseboat; Wolff and Elene within the car. As Newcombe states, in the dramatic form "perfected by television, we concentrate on the crucial human problems of individuals."[17] The smallness of television, if capitalized upon, can make us more aware of private moments, as when Vandam must admit to his son that Tobruk has fallen, and so sheds a tear.

This is not to suggest that the made-for-television movie is without problems or the novel without strengths. There are perhaps three areas in which the film adaptation is not entirely successful.

In the area of casting, the visual representation by an actor may or may not increase our understanding or appreciation of the story as a whole. David Soul, as the German spy, brings an appropriate physical bearing to the part and rounds out the characterization through tormented side-long glances after each killing. Cliff Robertson, on the other hand, while convincing as a middle-aged man reflecting on life's failures, seems awkward on a motorcycle and as the romantic lead.

Second, dialogue which is meant to be read cannot always be communicated orally. This is especially the case given the casting limitations imposed by a television budget. Several reviewers critiqued Robert Culp, who played Rommel, for his almost comical German accent, and the teleplay by Samuel Harris sometimes added anachronistic dialogue such as "Enjoy" and "You don't care about my needs." In addition, Cliff Robertson brought a flat, Midwestern tone to what had been an English part, and there is no explanation in the film as to why he and his son employ markedly different speech patterns.

Last, in the novel, the inner life of the characters sometimes added a dimension that was missing on the screen. For example, in one of the more interesting shifts in point-of-view in the book, Follett describes the belly dancer's perceptions of her audience and turns the entire section into a reflection on sexual control and power. Since film tends to deal with visuals and externals, these nuances are lost and the belly-dancing scenes become instead "titillating," in the words of one reviewer, and the stuff of "a highly commercial mini-series," in the opinion of another.[18]

Given the competent directing, however, this difference between fiction and film is actually capitalized upon and turned to advantage: At the same time that a more contemporary depiction of an empowered woman is lost, the made-for-televison movie gains through the recognition that it is part of a long line of spectacle films.

"Film," Robert Richardson tells us, "from its earliest days, has been aware of and quick to exploit its capacity to present spectacle," and the television version of *The Key to Rebecca* seems to draw from such Biblical epics as "Samson and Delilah" (1951), "The Ten Commandments" (1956), and "Cleopatra" ([1963]; Season Hubley's wig, the bubble bath scene, and various shots of Anthony Quayle as a kind of pasha on a couch, in particular), thus heightening the historical pageant latent in the novel.[19] In this sense, the television version comments directly on the book, recognizing the varied strains and attempting to resolve them in filmic terms.

Although there is some effort to resolve the Biblical epic and the espionage tale through costuming and symbolic actions, the ending is not entirely successful: Major Vandam, now robed like one of the twelve apostles, shoots the bearded Alex Wolff. His head bloodied, his sides pierced, Wolff struggles to carry a large radio transmitter hidden in a suitcase. He drops his "cross," then falls down, arms outstretched. But the other types of stories still require separate endings—one for the war epic, another for the love story, and so forth. On balance, however, the film version "The Key to Rebecca" was considered better-than-average television fare and was called "a worthy entry in the cinema spy genre."[20]

Other television adaptations of Follett novels have not been as favorably received. The 1994 version of *Lie Down with Lions* was termed "flat, uninspired and grueling, not to mention stylistically amateurish and dated," and while the 1996 adaptation of *The Third Twin* contained some interesting filmic moments (there is even a visual gag where Follett, in a brief cameo appearance, plays the servant "Ken"), those were primarily in the first half. As one television critic put it, "'The Third Twin' almost sinks under its own weight, and the more complex the storyline becomes, the more befuddled is the viewer."[21]

What is perhaps most intriguing about the television version of *The Third Twin* is the way in which the American production team softened the blatant ideology expressed in the novel.

Follett has acknowledged that his views on socialism are well known, at least in Europe,[22] and he has appeared on the American talk show "Politically Incorrect" as a representative from the Left. In *The Third Twin,* the evil triumvirate behind the cloning conspiracy are, of course, all middle-aged, white, male, upper-middle-class, card-carrying members of the G.O.P. The sympathetic characters in the novel, naturally enough, are either poor, women, minorities, students, or gays.

This heavy-handedness extends to the types of scenes that are created for polemical purposes: Steve Logan, a law student and one of the clones, decides that he must defend "the underdog against the injustice of a mighty institution" (303) because he has seen first-hand the corruption of the American criminal justice system. The principal linguistic device to shape readers' impressions is the use of highly connotative language: Steve notices while in jail that some prisoners "were apathetic and compliant, others loudly protested their innocence, and one struggled with the cops and got professionally beaten up as a result" (140)—a sentence which uses toneless Latinates for the oppressed, and sarcastic slang terms for the oppressors.

In the made-for-television version, not only is Steve's long ordeal at the hands of the police hardly shown, but almost entirely omitted are the book's references to political party affiliation (a brief visual reference to Richard Nixon is attached to a minor character toward the end of the film), and completely gone are the issues of a woman's freedom to choose marriage, an abortion, or some other arrangement, which were central themes in the novel. In addition, the iconography of the film—its use of casting, costuming, makeup, and sets—considerably undercuts the political outlook expressed in the written text.

Both Kelly McGillis, who plays the resilient university researcher, and Larry Hagman, who portrayed the corrupt administrator, bring a changed physical bearing to the part than is suggested by the novel. In the story, Jeannie Ferrami is described as a pugnacious, muscular tennis player, twenty-nine years old, who wears a pin in her nose and an orange jacket. The casting of an older actress added believability to the classroom lecture scenes, and the conservative makeup, dress, pants suit, and earrings become codes for conventionality (though a rose tatoo on her ankle is shown once, briefly).

In the novel, the university administrator, Berrington Jones, is proud of his association with Richard Nixon, Newt Gingrich, and Rush Limbaugh. In the television film, the casting, makeup, and hairstyle of Larry Hagman become visual parallels with another public figure—Bill Clinton. Larry Hagman's eyebrows have even been combed-out in imitation of the President's, and in the final scene he uses Clinton-like gestures and intonations during a press conference.

Other changes small and large are crafted into the television movie in order to dilute the ideology. One of the novel's African-American characters, Mr. Oliver, is changed to an elderly white man in the film, and Jeannie's censorious bourgeois sister does not appear at all. In fact, the interior set design for Jeannie's townhouse now suggests middle-class comfort for her as well, which eliminates the social class issues that were part of the text. Above all, the novel's verbal irony is missing from the film and while many of the more didactic scenes are retained—the break-in to the Pentagon, the sexual exploitation of the Asian maid, the smug celebration of the triumvirate—the sometimes unsubtle author-ial guidance is omitted, thus toning down those same scenes.

A final point about the adaptive process should be made: the fact that "The Key to Rebecca," "Lie Down with Lions," and "The Third Twin" were all intended for the small screen rather than for the large. In the previous chapter, we saw that the compression required by a two-hour film had worked against the expansion of plot, character, and tex-ture which had made *Eye of the Needle* a successful literary and popular piece. A central innovation in the made-for-television movie is the avoidance of the two-hour time-frame.

As a result, there are many serious and popular novelists who have noted the advantages of television adaptation over film: Larry McMurty, for example, calls the television mini-series ideal for novels with extended time spans, and James Michener has argued that a good book may become even better when serialized on television.[23] At the same time that compression and reduction inevitably take place through the process of dramatization, a broader and deeper examination of characters and themes may occur in a three- or four-hour television film. New-combe argues that because of such factors, the real relationship between the television mini-series and other art forms "lies not in movies or in radio, but in the novel. . . . Details take on importance slowly, and within repeated patterns of action, rather than with the immediacy of other visual forms."[24]

Follett has also concluded that although "The Key to Rebecca" was produced "for something like five or six million, which is very little for a mini-series[,] I thought they did a pretty good job. I prefer the quality you get filming for television; you have more time to develop character." The irony, therefore, is that while Follett's fiction may be more inher-ently suited to the small screen, he has also maintained that "for selling books, which is the real point of these things, feature films are better. They have a longer run and get more promotion."[25]

7

THE ART OF THE FIRST CHAPTER

"In the case of the six books that begin with *Eye of the Needle* and finish with *Lie Down with Lions,* I have looked for that rather rare situation in which an individual spy or secret agent could have done something which might have changed the course of history," Follett observed in a 1989 interview,[1] grouping together five thriller novels and one nonfiction book from his "middle period."

But many reviewers made distinctions between the works, noting for example that "Follett's first book—'Eye of the Needle'—was very good . . . skillful, suspenseful, visceral. But his second novel—'Triple' —was less good, and his [next] 'Key to Rebecca'—was burdened with cliché and coincidence."[2]

The critical opinion on three of those six books—*Triple* (1979), *The Key to Rebecca* (1980), and *Lie Down with Lions* (1985)—has been especially mixed, with some observers commenting on *Triple*'s "disjointed, tedious recounting" of a 1968 incident, on *The Key to Rebecca* as a thriller which is "decidedly second rate," and on *Lie Down with Lions* as a book that "buries probably scrupulous research under numbing prose." But many reviewers have also noted the engaging premise of those works; Roderick MacLeish terming Follett "a master of appropriate settings," and Andrew and Gina Macdonald acknowledging the novelist's conceptual "understanding of and tolerance for paradox and ambiguity." Even in a hostile and unnecessarily snide review of *The Key to Rebecca,* Peter Andrews of the *New York Times* grudgingly admitted that "the story could have been a good one."[3]

Interestingly, Andrews, in the 1980 review which understandably rankled Follett, did note the technical skill in the early pages: "As in *Eye of the Needle,* he starts out with a sensational first chapter; [but] it is largely the same chapter written all over again in a different setting."[4]

As we shall see in the following pages, Follett's concern with the careful construction of compelling first chapters may well be the result of literary and commercial currents facing writers at the time when he was first publishing. His emphasis on the maintenance of pace has been noted elsewhere in this study, as has his reliance on an extensive and detailed outline. Follett has also indicated that he is an impatient reader of other people's thrillers: "I've become very intolerant in fiction. Many, many books I read just a few pages, 10 pages, 50 pages and stop."[5] Perhaps as a result of his own reader impatience, many of his first chapters thus seem deliberately designed to be "grabbers" and make use of the classic elements of effective short stories: setting, plot, characterization, tone, irony, and symbol.

"Readers [may] not notice such things," he pointed out in reference to careful chapter construction, "but still I suspect that regularity, and even [chapter] symmetry, contribute to what they perceive as a well-told story."[6]

Since Follett is primarily a novelist, however, his experience with the short story form has been limited. He sold "one or two" in the 1970s "but nothing much came of them." He published a category romance short story in 1990 and, significantly, the first chapters from *The Key to Rebecca* and *Lie Down with Lions* have appeared in popular magazines and have been indexed as short stories.[7]

In both literary and mass-market magazines, first chapters are sometimes presented as a unique art form—as succinct and self-contained as the short stories published next to them. The opening pages of Follett's three Middle Eastern novels stand as classic examples of the art of the first chapter: the initial use of irony in *Lie Down with Lions*, the integration of literary elements in *The Key to Rebecca*, and the inclusion of a fairy tale subtext in *Triple*. Although the novels themselves never fulfill the promise of their openings, these three chapters can be studied on their own as if they were short stories, especially since in the first, irony yields to the demands of formula; in the second, literary elements result in the expression of theme; and in the third, folk tale qualities convey psychological meaning.

Irony, it can be said, is at the heart of fiction. The author's ironic tone or deliberate contrasting of what seems and what is, allows readers to recognize the heightened and invented qualities that make it fiction and make it different from the "true account."

The first chapter of *Lie Down with Lions* focuses on a successful sting operation against a terrorist group in Paris. The complication for the C.I.A. operative, Ellis Thaler, is that his work assignments take him away from the woman he wants to marry, Jane Lambert.

Both plot lines—the counterterrorist measures and the human interest story—could be factual incidents from different sections of a newspaper, but their treatment—and their intersection—make them the stuff of fiction.

In the first place, the opening paragraphs of *Lie Down with Lions* employ a rhetorical mode reminiscent of E. M. Forster's "irony tempered with vision and prophecy."[8] Not only are there frequent authorial asides ("for—as he cheerfully admitted—'Idealists pay higher prices'" [3]), which comment on the irony of situations ("They chose Yilmaz as their next target because he was a wealthy supporter of the military dictatorship and because he lived, conveniently, in Paris" [3]), but specific incongruities seem deliberately worked in: the short-lived, revolutionary newspaper, for example, is entitled *Chaos* or the gangster wears "a black suit as if he had been to Mass, which he probably had" (14). Above all, the early use of narrative summary in this chapter results in authorial distance, even when reporting dialogue:

> There was one more snag.
> I've got a friend, Rahmi said, who wants to meet you both, Ellis and Pepe. To tell you the truth he *must* meet you . . . for this is the friend who gives us the money for explosives and cars and bribes and guns and everything.
> Why does he want to meet us? Ellis and Pepe wanted to know. (7)

The indirect discourse, in fact, allows for an omniscient point-of-view and a slightly whimsical tone, as in the humorously extended list of items the money is used for. But this technique, and the promise of a literary tone, is abandoned within a few pages for an approach which has been imbedded in magazine stories for more than a century—the reliance on a single point-of-view and directly dramatized scenes.

Edgar Allan Poe, who has been credited with developing the modern short story, also established the theory of "the single effect." A generation later, in a seminal essay entitled "The Philosophy of the Short Story" (1901), Brander Matthews attempted to codify Poe's theories: "A Short-story," Matthews wrote, "deals with a single character, a single event, a single emotion, or the series of emotions called forth by a single situation."[9] Within three pages, the point of view in the first chapter of *Lie Down with Lions* moves into a single character's consciousness and remains there in adherence to the rules established by Matthews and others over a long period of time.

Between 1900 and 1950 the numerous short story "how to's" which gained popularity among aspiring writers also exerted an inescapable influence on commercial short fiction. Charles E. May, in a useful survey of such manuals, argues that the various practical "guides for writers" had a lamentable yet enduring effect on the short story form as it developed up to about 1970, not only solidifying it by rules and tainting it by commercialization, but also sharpening the division between the quality literary story, which he termed psychological and poetic, and the formula commercial story, which he quoted as a "'fable founded on sentimental mottoes.'"[10]

During the period leading up to Follett's emergence as a writer, an understanding of popular formulaic conventions would be essential for anyone who wanted to write for *Collier's, Esquire* or, for that matter, *Cosmopolitan*—the outlet for the first chapter of *Lie Down with Lions.* As Ian Hamilton has observed, "no aspiring pro . . . could afford to despise" such manuals altogether (63), and he mentions Jack Woodford's *Trial and Error* in particular as "a standard how-to text for up-and-coming pros" in the 1930s and 1940s.[11]

Follett, growing up a generation later and on the other side of the Atlantic, may never have read such a manual but the countless short story writers who did and who followed its tenets set the tone and style for the commercial magazine story.

The first chapter of *Lie Down with Lions,* with its lengthy passages of direct discourse, is a case in point. When asked in a television interview if his books were "driven by dialogue" because dialogue was easier to write, Follett explained that "[i]t's much more natural to tell the story in terms of people talking, just as we're talking now, rather than to have the narrator, as it were, the author, say what happened. It makes it more immediate." But in relying on dialogue to create scenes, Follett is also adhering to the established commercial short story pattern described by Woodford: "A [short] story that is 75 per cent dialogue is at least ten times as easy to sell as one that is 50 per cent dialogue. . . . NEVER have less than 25 per cent dialogue."[12]

Structurally, too, the first chapter of *Lie Down with Lions* seems consistent with the formula story. Ideally, Woodford maintains, a writer should *begin* a story with "the bit you originally thought was its middle—you should go from the middle to the beginning to the end,"[13] as Follett does when he writes the very first line of the chapter—"The men who wanted to kill Ahmet Yilmaz were serious people" (3), thus anticipating the turning point of the chapter when the conspiracy is foiled.

For other reasons as well, the first chapter of *Lie Down with Lions* reads like a generic short story. To cite Matthews, the "solidifier" of this form:

A true Short Story differs from the Novel chiefly in its essential unity of impression. . . . [Often] the Short Story fulfils the three false unities of the French classic drama: it shows one action, in one place, on one day.[14]

This first chapter concludes its action "at the end of the day" (*Lie Down* 6), takes place "in the vicinity of the Champs-Élysées" (20), and can end when the dramatic question posed early in the chapter has been answered, thus preserving a strict unity of action.[15]

In standard short story form, therefore, this dramatic question is both external—will Ellis foil the plot?—as well as internal—will he express his feelings for Jane?—and the climax is resolved first externally and then internally. The very last line of the chapter has Ellis stating that he is going to "tell her I catch terrorists for a living and ask her to marry me" (22).

The opening chapter of *The Key to Rebecca* and the beginning of *Triple* share this structural completeness, this "unity of impression" and effect with *Lie Down with Lions,* but differ in style and approach in a number of significant ways.

For example, *The Key to Rebecca* represents a return to the same World War II setting of *Eye of the Needle* and, to a certain extent, to its fuller literary texture. This is especially apparent in the first chapter, which is written in narrative exposition, rather than with dialogue, and which uses detailed paragraphs, complex sentence patterns and elevated diction fully merged to point-of-view:

The jeep drove through the busy, narrow streets. The familiar sights of an Egyptian town pleased Wolff: the gay cotton clothes, the women carrying bundles on their heads, the officious policemen, the sharp characters in sunglasses, the tiny shops spilling out into the rutted streets, the stalls, the battered cars and the overloaded asses. They stopped in front of a row of low mud-brick buildings. The road was half blocked by an ancient truck and the remains of a cannibalized Fiat. A small boy was working on a cylinder block with a wrench, sitting on the ground outside the entrance. (14)

The fullness is in part achieved through the extended list, which, unlike other passages cited in chapter 6 of this study, follow directly from character—from what pleased Wolff. In addition, there is the generally slower pacing of scenes, allowing for moment-by-moment depiction of small actions, such as the boy working on the cylinder block.

Although A. J. Mayer, in reviewing *The Key to Rebecca,* concluded that on balance "Follett is no literary stylist," in this first chapter, at least, the inclusion of metaphor and personification, symbol and allusion, and the development of theme are present and are the elements that one would expect in a compressed if more literary short story—the type May categorizes as "psychological [and] poetic."[16]

The first chapter describes how Alex Wolff crosses the desert, despite the death of his camel, and is helped by Bedouins. He infiltrates the Allied lines and accepts a ride from a British corporal. When the corporal discovers forged banknotes in Wolff's suitcase, Wolff must kill him with a knife.

This straight-forward storyline is rendered with considerable literary texture. The desert is referred to as "the inconstant sand" and the camel stares out "with the indifference of the dying" (3). Wolff reads from Du Maurier's *Rebecca* (the title itself provides the central literary allusion), and he reflects that "[h]e would not wait for death. . . . Not for him the hours of agony and encroaching madness" (6), an observation which seems a blend of Emily Dickinson and William Wordsworth.[17] But it is in the use of concrete symbol that theme is developed, giving this first chapter a unity and cohesion perhaps not present in the novel overall.

Theme is the combination of all the formal elements, starting perhaps with setting and its direct influence on character. When the first sentence of the chapter reads: "The camel collapsed at noon," the dramatic question is implied—would the rider collapse as well in this hostile wartime place? The emphasis on the camel as a symbol of indifference toward death is used to establish a central contrast with the man, who is determined to "set his strength and expertise against the ruthless desert" (6). His character is established as in conflict with the locale since he rejects the camel's "tranquility of exhaustion" when facing death, yet wonders "if the desert would win" (6).

This leads him to a reflection on the landscape, which is described as both threatening and purifying, as a place where "the moon went down, but the landscape was bright with starlight" (6) and where the contrast between light and dark, between destruction and survival, is remembered in knife-like terms, as a "gorgeous sunrise like a straight rainbow against the flat black horizon" and as an "icy morning wind [that] blew into his face" (6).

Later in the chapter, animals like the camel are increasingly identified with this central contrast between destruction and survival, between the meek and the mighty. Near the nomads' camp, sheep graze in a flock and the camels, which also search for food, are "hobbled" (8). The sight of the camels prompts the man, Wolff, to question whether he has the needed cruelty to survive in the desert in wartime: He wonders whether he should have "lit a fire underneath his dying white [camel] yesterday? [The nomad] would have" (8).

The name "Wolff," of course, represents a predatory animal and in an earlier version of the text the spy's name was apparently "Webb" (suggesting "ensnared" or "entrapped").[18] The name change seems deliberate and significant, and through it the duality of the character and his relationship to the classic spy formula is clarified: a "Wolff" is both hunter and hunted.

This duality is again emphasized through reference to animals: Wolff "always did believe in the desert lion[s]" who, like the Germans, "are proud, and cruel, and strong. . . . It was possible [that] a few of [the lions] remained, hiding in the mountains, living off deer and fennec fox and wild sheep" (9), and it is through these parallels and through his Arab friend's repeated references to the atmosphere of war that the theme is clarified: In wartime, in order to survive, the individual must become fierce and animal-like, a predator. The dramatic question in the chapter, as in a tightly constructed short story, is also increasingly individualized: Is Wolff that sort of person?

In discussing the pattern of both psychological and formula short stories through the 1950s, Theodore Stroud wrote that:

[T]he completeness results from the units or episodes in a story being combined to make credible a 'change' in one of the characters. And all the episodes in such stories, upon consideration, appear to bear upon this change, either as weakening or as strengthening his resistance to becoming a person perceptibly different from what he was in the beginning.[19]

Such a pattern clearly underlies Follett's first chapter design in *The Key to Rebecca,* since every moment, including the numerous references to ritual washing and symbolic purification, trace in a change and show how in each scene Wolff is that much closer to answering the dramatic question for himself. First, he must transform his self-image, through "a little water in a bowl," and then shave so that "[g]radually his old face emerged" (10). Next, he must dress in Western clothing and re-adopt his old identity: "he realized that once again he was Alexander Wolff, age thirty-four, of Villa les Oliviers, Garden City, Cairo, a businessman, race—European" (11) so that he might survive behind British lines.

Writing a few years before the publication of these novels, Richard Kostelanetz pointed out that in the ideal structure of a short story, "each new paragraph should offer a succession of surprises or intensifying symbols" so that "the story becomes an elaboration of the opening elements."[20] With each succeeding incident in the first chapter of *The Key to Rebecca,* the dramatic question, which has grown out of the very first line of the book, is rephrased in increasingly pointed terms: were Wolff's senses alert to the right things? (12); would he save himself from error? (15); was he thinking hard enough or fast enough? (14); would his plan of slipping into Egypt fail? (15).

Toward the end of the chapter the implied questions come with increasing rapidity, creating a rising "pattern of expectation . . . concluded by the story's logical end."[21] When Wolff is able to kill, viciously, and cruelly by using a "wicked curved Bedouin knife," he has been pushed by the setting and the wartime circumstances into what he realizes is "increasingly senseless behavior" (16). The final line of the chapter demonstrates his complete transformation and answers the dramatic question: in killing he feels "nothing, only disappointment" (17) and has become the true predator that can survive.

It is this focus on internal change and on psychological motivation which makes the chapter verge on the literary; and it is this succinctness and control, derived in part from the commercial short story pattern, which makes a "short story [come] near to being a lyric."[22]

But by far, the most complete example of a first chapter which reads like a tale (the oldest definition of a short story) is in *Triple*.

The initial pages recount the arrival in Oxford of Al Cortone, an ex-G.I. who has come to look up an old friend, Nat Dickstein. The two talk about their experiences together in Italy during World War II and discuss Nat's present love interest, Mrs. Ashford, who is also a professor's wife.

Later that same morning, Nat and Al attend a sherry party hosted by the Ashfords and meet a third individual, Yasif Hassan.

At the party, Nat is treated like a son by Professor Ashford but is shocked when he later sees his "beloved" in the arms of his rival.

As we shall see, this storyline contains the qualities of the fable and its treatment results in a totality of effect. In a famous review of Hawthorne's *Twice-Told Tales,* Edgar Allan Poe explained the effect of "totality" essential to the traditional short story form:

A skillful artist has constructed a tale. He has not fashioned his thoughts to accommodate his incidents, but having deliberately conceived a certain single effect to be wrought, he then invents such incidents, he then combines such events, and discusses them in such a tone as may best serve him in establishing this preconceived effect.[23]

Triple begins with the voice of the folklorist: "There was a time, just once, when they were all together,"[24] which not only establishes that this opening section may be preconceived to have the completeness of the folk-fairy tale, but may be designed to have a similar psychological impact. The fairy tale often leads to a sudden reversal of the beginning situation and may have as its subtext some sexual or separation anxiety. In other words, as Poe stated, if the writer's "very first sentence tend not to the out-bringing of [an] effect, then in his very first step he has committed a blunder."[25]

Follett builds his chapter with a completeness not always present elsewhere: he tells us, still with the voice of the folklorist, that "the whole day [would become] so important, twenty-one years later" and that this "early meeting [was] a coincidence [though] they were destined to have power . . . each in their different ways, in their different countries" (1), thus creating anticipation and suggesting the inevitability of separation. The brief prologue concludes with a direct statement forecasting the end: "It was an uneventful occasion. Well, almost" (1), so that readers will know that the chapter will turn on an event, something which will change characters as fundamentally as Joyce's characters are changed by their "epiphanies" and akin to the psychological or sexual crises imbedded in the fairy tale.

Oedipal conflicts abound in the chapter, as they do in many fairy tales: the central character, Nat Dickstein, has had his leg broken repeatedly and, as we have noted, is in love with his professor's wife. "She's out of reach" (5), he tells his friend, Al Cortone, and is described as "blushing" and "embarrassed" (5). Although the chapter is told from Cortone's point-of-view, which allows for some authorial distance and irony, the focus is really on Dickstein and on what Matthews calls "a single character, a single event, a single emotion or series of emotions called forth by a single situation."

He is depicted as child-like, not just because of his infatuation with Professor Ashford's wife, who refers to him as "only a boy" (9), but in his laughter (7) and in his awkwardness when Cortone indulges in sexual innuendo (3). Dickstein's name, of course, suggests male sexual arousal and the chapter initially misdirects the reader to believe that the sexual rivalry is between Dickstein and the effete father-figure, Professor Ashford, "[a] middle-aged man in baggy trousers" who is "balding" and who brushes "nervously at the wispy hair behind his ears" (9-11), but who treats Nat kindly. Dickstein's alter-ego, the coarse extrovert Cortone, tells Nat that he doesn't believe "Mrs. Ashford is out of reach" (12), the reference to her married name establishing her as a mother-surrogate despite her youth, and moments before the surprise revelation and its "effect of totality," Nat is again completely identified with the child—in fact, with the Ashford's daughter, so that he becomes another offspring in the context of the Ashford home: "[He] was kneeling down and stroking the cat. Nat and Suza appeared to be pals" (12).

Once this Oedipal triangle between Professor Ashford, his wife, and Nat has been made complete (the title *Triple* referring as effectively to the first chapter as to the novel itself), the chapter can close according to its pre-established design: the child will witness a primal scene—the parents making love—and will experience feelings of sexual betrayal and anger: "Dickstein's face was gray with shock, and he looked ill; his mouth dropped open as he gazed with horror and despair" (13).

The shock for the reader, the "idea of the tale," as Poe puts it, is that there is another side to the triangle, an additional reversal when "the false hero or villain is exposed"[26]—the true sexual rival is not Professor Ashford but another student, Yasif Hassan, one of those who had been at the meeting, "just once, when they were all together" (*Triple* 1). The unity which had been established in the very first sentence of the chapter is now broken and, in the words of Poe, "[t]he idea of the tale, its thesis, has been presented unblemished, because undisturbed—an end demanded, yet, in the novel, altogether unattainable."[27]

8

UNIFICATION AND EVAPORATION
IN *THE MAN FROM ST. PETERSBURG*

Throughout this study, we have alluded to Follett's ability to blend different types of stories into a hybrid form—in many instances, in the attempt to expand his readership. We have also seen that this process of "hybridization" sometimes resulted in highly successful, and at other times in less-than-fully successful end products. Yet underlying almost all of Follett's work is a basic combination of romance elements with adventure story motifs.

We have also considered some of the various cultural influences on his writing, from popular films to hard-boiled detective novels to social realist work. But the biggest-selling writer in Britain in the 1980s was not Follett, whose works have never sold particularly well in his own country, but the "Queen of Romance"—Barbara Cartland, who by 1982 had written 362 books, most of them romance novels, and had sold more than 350 million copies worldwide. In America, as well, category romance novels were a startling cultural and publishing phenomenon, with Harlequin Books alone selling over 200 million books in a single year.[1]

Writing for *The Dictionary of Literary Biography* in 1981, Michael Adams observed that Follett is "a calculating surveyor of the mass-market [who] also realizes that while loyal spy-novel readership is predominantly male, female readers are needed, as they always have been, to insure best-sellers." His works were also called a "variation upon history,"[2] but up until that point his three novels which could be considered "historical"—*Eye of the Needle, Triple,* and *The Key to Rebecca*—had all been set in the recent or fairly recent past. For his readers in the late 1970s and early 1980s, this was especially the case with *Triple,* in which the main events take place in 1968.

The first novel that could have been considered genuinely historical by a majority of his readers was *The Man from St. Petersburg,* published in 1981 but set in the days leading up to the First World War. Responding to the cultural currents of the 1980s, however, *The Man from St. Petersburg* derives as many of its conventions from the category romance as it does from the spy thriller.

Initially, this would seem a highly unusual pairing of two presumably very different types of mass-market literature, and it is worth considering the connections between the romance novel and the espionage story in some detail. First, what are the defining similarities and differences between these two forms? Second, how does Follett apply the conventions of the romance to amend the spy story? And third, does a recognition of melodrama, in the best and the worst senses of the term, give Follett a larger category with which to unify the text?

A number of culture critics writing in the early 1980s, as well as publishers' submission guidelines and the books themselves, help us define the type of category-romance story that had such a vast following a decade ago. In essence, the category romance is a love story that focuses on a single male-female relationship, yet often uses character-foils as false but ultimately unacceptable alternatives. Through a central female consciousness, the story concentrates on the working out of that love relationship toward a happy ending.

In many instances, the conflict in such formula stories revolves around the young woman's desire to convince the older, often aristocratic but always successful older male that her world of love should triumph over his world of things: in other words, the novel details a sensitizing process. While numerous critics of the form have commented on the folk-tale subtext, especially the Cinderella myth and the Beggarman and the Princess tale, Janice Radway, in her pioneering work *Reading the Romance* (1984), argues that the "fairy-tale union of the hero and the heroine is in reality the symbolic fulfillment of a woman's desire to realize her most basic self in relation with another."[3] Thus, the romance story actually describes a drive toward the nurturing and the need to be nurtured as well as the heroine's search for a true parental figure; that is to say, maternal figure, in Radway's view.

The quest for completion and the symbolic search for a parent is a frequent element in the other category from which Follett draws: the male-oriented spy thriller. John Cawelti and Bruce A. Rosenberg, in their study *The Spy Story,* identify several familiar patterns common to the spy thriller, from assassination to confrontation to betrayal.[4] While such episodes may be found in mysteries as well, in the context of the espionage story these familiar patterns become *familial.*

For example, in James Carroll's *Family Trade,* which was published the same year as *The Man from St. Petersburg,* the hero is a young man who has grown up in the shadow of his superspy father. The son's quest takes on multiple yet interconnected goals: he must prove that his father did not betray his country and his mother; he must prove to himself that he is as good as his parent.

In other spy novels from the Cold War era, ranging from Len Deighton's *The Ipcress File* (1962) to Charles McCarry's *The Miernick Dossier* (1973), a central intrigue relates to the trustworthiness of the Control, who can be seen as both father-figure and adversary. The frequent use of assassination as a trope in espionage novels—the killing of a father-figure—suggests that such Oedipal rivalries are an important ingredient in the form.

An even more explicit example of such anxieties is in a short story entitled "The Mentor" which appeared in a mass-market magazine from the 1980s. In the story, the relationship between spy and control has "more than once been likened to a father's and son's. Trego, years ago, had even heard unconfirmed whispers that the Essex estate had been willed to him." The father-figure, Essex, ends up killing Trego and then waits for new "sons" to come visit him.[5]

We can establish other clear parallels between the spy novel and the woman's romance. In either category, paranoia looms large. Tania Modleski, in her study of mass-produced fantasies for women, argues that male figures in romance novels are portrayed as both enemies and lovers and that the "Gothic Romance" sub-category in particular expresses an extreme fear: "'pure Gothics,'" she cites an editor as noting, "almost always have 'a handsome, magnetic suitor or husband who may or may not be a lunatic and/or murderer'[, and] one is struck by the strong element of paranoia."[6]

In the spy thriller, this fear extends beyond the domestic enclave and becomes a fear of the larger world itself. In novel after novel, we find a fundamental ingredient: the spy/hunter finds himself hunted by his own agency, several foreign networks, his enemies, and at times even people he had thought were his friends. As Richard Hannay states in *The 39 Steps,* a work that established "a pattern for adventure-writers ever since"[7]—"I reckoned that two sets of people would be out looking for me—Scudder's enemies to put me out of existence, and the police, who would want me for murder. It was going to be a giddy hunt and it was queer how the prospect comforted me." This atmosphere of paranoia is central to the thriller, according to Jerry Palmer, and distinguishes the genre from other closely related forms.[8]

Where the spy story and the category romance diverge, however, is in two key areas: first of all, the element of suspense is handled differently by thriller and romance writers. In the spy story, the exact nature of the conspiracy is not known until the very end, and adds to a sense of danger. In the romance, the reader understands from the very first what the two lovers must discover on their own: that they are right for each other. The question in the romance is not what is behind it all, but how and when the union will occur.

Second, the two forms express contrasting attitudes toward power and the world of things. Palmer and others have pointed to "the instinctive competitive personality" of the spy hero and the fundamental fantasy appeal to its male readers: the thriller is the story of a man on an important mission who is good at his job. In the romance story, on the other hand, competition and public achievement are ultimately devalued. As Modleski notes, "the man is brought to acknowledge the preeminence of love and the attractions of domesticity, at which he has, as a rule, previously scoffed."[9]

This contrast between internal and external worlds clarifies the most fundamental way in which the two genres stand in opposition. "The other woman" in the romance story is a rival precisely because she is materialistic and competitive. Radway points out that "the female foil's self-interested pursuit of a comfortable social position" shows that she is "incapable of caring for anyone,"[10] and such novels, on balance, celebrate the triumph of love over things.

In Graham Greene's *The Human Factor,* the agent Maurice Castle is compromised at the exact moment when he places love above duty to the organization, and in other espionage stories, such as Ian Fleming's James Bond series, sexual involvements are not only temporary, but connections to the father-figure are frequently broken off as well. As a result, fear in the spy story becomes a fear of a public threat—the conspiracy, which will eventually be controlled—and of private, domestic entanglements, which must be avoided at all costs. Graham Greene, in fact, chooses to quote Joseph Conrad's Axel Heyst—a man who wished to live alone—for the epigraph to *The Human Factor:* "I only know that he who forms a tie is lost. The germ of corruption has entered into his soul."[11]

In *The Man from St. Petersburg,* Follett takes as an epigraph a statement by Graham Greene: "One can't love humanity. One can only love people,"[12] suggesting that the novel will be as much about love as about the abstractions of politics. In the novel, Follett applies many of the techniques of the category romance to soften the outlook of the political thriller, though at times this creates some contradictions.

In the summer of 1914, as Germany prepares for war, England is desperate to negotiate an alliance with Russia. A Russian, Prince Orlov, is sent to London to arrange the treaty but is trailed by Feliks Kschessinsky, an anarchist determined to assassinate him and save the lives of thousands of peasants.

Complications arise when the English representative at the negotiations, Lord Walden, turns out to be married to Orlov's aunt, who was also Kschessinsky's mistress.

Much of the novel is seen through the eyes of Lord Walden's daughter, a naive and inquisitive eighteen-year-old described in the formulaic phrasings of the romance novel: "Charlotte looked both beautiful and innocent—just the effect that was called for in the debutante" (37). The Silhouette tip sheets stipulate that the heroine "is almost always a virgin, young (19-29) [and] is basically an ingenue," and Radway notes that in the "ideal" romance novel preferred by the readers she surveyed, the heroine's sexual innocence, unselfconscious beauty, and independent spirit were highly valued traits.[13]

Charlotte becomes more independent through her political awakening and her defense of Feliks Kschessinsky, who turns out to be her biological father. In addition, Follett links her emerging sexual awareness to a growing political understanding, and this becomes one of the main themes of the book. Initially sheltered from many of the more revolutionary currents of the day—"the suffragettes, their hunger strikes, and the consequent forced feeding" (69), she later attends a violent political rally (189) and hides Kschessinsky in her bedroom (292).

Changed by these experiences, which have involved a search for a true father in order to validate her own identity, Charlotte, we are told in the epilogue, lives on to marry a committed socialist and pacifist and stays active in contemporary political causes.

Thus, the storyline in *The Man from St. Petersburg* bears only a surface resemblance to that of a spy story, with its enemy agent in hostile territory, its hunter/hunted motif, and its allusion to the game (as in Ks-*chess*-insky's name), and its various chases across a city. As T. J. Binyon noted in a *Times Literary Supplement* review, "[a]ction throughout takes second place to emotional and sexual entanglements, to complicated relationships between husband and wife, lover and mistress, father and daughter."[14] Charlotte is at the center of all these relationships, as "daughter" to the three other main characters.

Technically, the novel uses an omniscient point-of-view, shifting from character to character, but increasingly Charlotte's personal and political outlook comes to dominate. In a sense, by layering a strong female sensibility into the story of assassination and intrigue, the book devalues the world of achievement and power. Late in the novel:

[Charlotte] was desperate for him to understand. "I don't know whether [war] is evil, but I do know it's wrong. The Russian peasants know nothing of European politics, and they care less. But they will be shot to pieces and have their legs blown off and all awful things like that because you make an agreement with Alexs!" (310)

Not only do we find the breathless exclamations common to the narrative consciousness in the category romance, but the superiority of caring for people over caring for things is explicitly stated.

In other ways, too, the novel diminishes the world of power and politics and reinforces the view expressed by Charlotte. The treaty negotiations are depicted as a childish game, and unfavorable portraits of Churchill, Lloyd George, and Asquith show them to be infuriatingly "casual" about grave political decisions that will affect the lives of millions (251). As such, the novel represents not only the use of the characteristic romance sensibility, but an early example of Follett's revisionist approach to history and increasingly overt expression of Leftist ideology. Churchill, for example, is referred to as a "young demagogue [who] might have a brain" (7), and in an epilogue set in the present, Margaret Thatcher is dismissed as someone who has given "feminism a bad name" (342).

As with the romance novel, characters who are excessively concerned with social position and the trappings of wealth are used to highlight the more caring and decent qualities of the ingenue. Belinda, Charlotte's cousin and girlhood friend, is mostly interested in fashion and in attending society balls; Lydia, Charlotte's mother, who is also obsessed with appearances and with maintaining her own social status, becomes a kind of symbolic rival for the love of Feliks Kschessinsky, since Charlotte's biological father has developed an intense affection for Charlotte.

Not only must Charlotte eventually displace her rival for the love of a father-figure, but she must choose between true and false "suitors" herself. On the one hand, Lord Walden, the man who has raised her, can be steadfast and committed to duty; on the other, he is stuffily conventional and is also too concerned with appearances: "'Whether you realize this or not,'" he states, "'this episode is a social catastrophe for us all'" (259).

So, too, with Feliks: outwardly, he is appealing, with "a long face [and] curved nose" (193) and an intense gaze that Charlotte finds both compassionate and discomforting (193). Inwardly, Feliks is driven by hatred rather than by love, and he parallels the lunatic/lover of the Gothic romance when he thinks of telling a maid "'I am a madman, . . . but if you make me a sandwich I won't rape you'" (229).

Radway notes that the trajectory of the category romance involves "the heroine's transformation from an isolated, asexual, insecure adolescent who is unsure of her own identity, into a mature, sensual, and very married woman who has realized her full potential and identity as the partner of a man and as the implied mother of a child."[15] Charlotte is first presented as someone who is treated as a child and is only "occasionally permitted to put up her hair and dress for dinner" (15). Because of her insularity, she is exceptionally naive about sexual matters and must steal a home medical guide and a Victorian pornographic novel in the hopes of "discover[ing] the secret of life" (21). But by the middle of the novel, when told about the procreative act, "[i]t seemed, unaccountably, to make sense" (109). The epilogue confirms what the progress of the story had suggested, that Charlotte would marry and live comfortably and enjoy being "surrounded by people" (342).

The Man from St. Petersburg is, of course, not a "pure" romance since one of the defining qualities of that form is that the story must be "concerned with the development of true love with a view to marriage,"[16] but neither is it a "pure" espionage story. Perhaps a better label would be "romance melodrama." Avoiding the more common, pejorative sense of the term "melodrama," Cawelti has argued that popular melodramas are "the fantasy of the world that operates according to our heart's desires" where the whole world bears out "the audience's traditional patterns of right and wrong, good and evil." Because of this concern with the whole world and the need to reveal it as fundamentally fair, "melodramas are usually rather complicated in plot and characters. . . . Subplots multiply, and the point-of-view continually shifts in order to involve us in a complex of destinies" (45).

The attempt to blend two different categories, even under the heading of "melodrama," does create tensions within the text, but also the opportunity to resolve the inherent splits, doublings, and divisions that are found in most any allegorical form.

The principal dilemma in *The Man from St. Petersburg* results from combining the political ideology of the liberal spy novel[17] with the more conservative outlook of the 1980s' category romance. On one hand, those who are willing to fight for the rights of the poor are viewed as heroic in *The Man from St. Petersburg* (33). In contrast, the fantasy world of wealth is indulged in at the same time it is condemned: "The dress of white tulle embroidered with crystals, went down almost to the floor and partly covered the tiny pointed shoes. Its neckline, plunging to waist level," and so on (37)—a form of narcissism derived from the romance novel.

As with romance novels of a decade ago, *The Man from St. Petersburg* uses a female sensibility, but stops short of a full commitment to feminism. While the patriarchal social order is viewed as oppressive, having kept Charlotte in ignorance and Lydia in a passionless marriage, the novel—as with the mass-produced Silhouette and Harlequin fantasies—still argues that fulfillment can only come through domesticity:

"It was after the birth of Charlotte that everything settled down [for Lydia]. The servants adored the baby and loved Lydia for producing it" (298). The epilogue not only tells us that Charlotte's personal and political identity is equated with marriage, but that Lydia has had another child, bringing to a close her rebellion.

But the clearest example of the abandonment of revolutionary zeal for domestic union comes in the case of Feliks Kschessinsky. For 19 years he has been goaded by a single passion: the desire to destroy an unjust system. A relentless killer of the police and of other "class traitors," he is suddenly softened by the discovery of his own fatherhood:

Feliks could not stop crying. . . . People stared at him as he walked through the park [shaking] with uncontrollable sobs and with tears pouring down his face . . . She's so beautiful, he thought. But he was not weeping for what he had found; he was weeping for what he had lost. (214)

Although the sensitizing of male characters is an important ingredient in the category romance novel, by tying that element so completely to political values, Follett actually diminishes the importance of the ideology he might wish to espouse.

But there are other kinds of splits and divisions within the novel that can be more fully addressed by familiar means: by the confrontation, purgation and reintegration of a divided self common to melodrama.

From the very beginning "duality" has figured prominently in the novel, not just because of the social class divisions or the political divide facing a Europe on the brink of war, but also because of the polarities of restraint and freedom that the novel suggests lie within each individual. Charlotte, for example, thinks of herself as having a "Jekyll and Hyde" personality as she moves between the sexual repression of the day and her innate curiosity (257). Feliks, as well, is torn by his awakened feelings of affection and his bonds to political reform.

The doubling of characters, of course, is used as it always has been in melodrama—to demonstrate the differences between virtue and villainy and to dramatize the moral choices each individual must make. As with Feliks, the biological father, Lord Walden, the father by law, must also decide between the call of duty and the ties of feeling. What, in the classic espionage story would most likely be seen as a fatal mistake—the forming of a tie—in *The Man from St. Petersburg* suggests that Walden will be the better parent. Unlike Feliks, who ultimately decides that "his feelings [for Charlotte] were ridiculous" when compared to the chance to "spark the Russian Revolution" (226), Walden impulsively declares that he places Charlotte "above all principles, all politics, everything" (311). In romance-novel format, the test of authenticity in the suitor is his ability to feel.

Charlotte is doubled with Lydia, who also moves between repression and freedom and who compares herself to her daughter at that same age. And as with "the other woman" in the romance novel who "flaunt[s] her sexual availability,"[18] Lydia is the extreme counterpart of the heroine. Charlotte's virginity is contrasted with Lydia's voracious hungers and lack of control (she even uses opium). Both women want Feliks in a special way, and in those scenes in which Lydia or Charlotte are alone with him, the writing makes use of formulaic love-story clichés:

Lydia, for instance, remembers Feliks as having "the face of a wolf and the eyes of a spaniel . . . thin as a rail . . . and he had clever, clever hands" (11). The animal imagery, the allusiveness, and the repetitive phrasing are stylistic techniques common to category romance writers. Just as importantly, these are all genre images for passion, and Lydia will later be revealed as the false partner because of excessive behavior.

Charlotte's encounters with Feliks also rely on the diction of the love story: "Her young face was so grave that he held her hand. . . . [Charlotte said,] 'So I'll never see you again'" (304), but the statements, while sentimental and familiar, emphasize the essential purity of the heroine and place her in stark contrast with her foil.

The love between Charlotte and Feliks cannot be consummated in any physical sense, and yet the form, at least as stipulated by the Silhouette tip sheets, demands that "love scenes be frequent and escalate in intensity."[19] Melodrama, however, allows for stock figures and for ritualized actions that become clearly representational. Lydia, as a surrogate for Charlotte, *may* consummate the requisite union with Feliks, and the novel points directly to this more symbolic, representational level. Not only has Feliks equated Lydia and Charlotte through their laughter (196), but the bedroom's candlelight transforms Lydia into a youth. We are told that "Lydia *was* nineteen again" (316 [emphasis added]). More significantly, the act takes place in Charlotte's own bedroom where Feliks has felt "very strange . . . in the place where Charlotte had spent so many hours of her childhood" (315). Obviously, more than a simple social code has been broken. While the category romance of the 1980s seldom deals with the taboo of incest or, at one time, of miscegenation, 19th-century melodrama often does. As a result, punishment for the false hero and heroine who have broken with societal norms must be according to the demands of melodrama, not romance.

The love story needs merely to reject the false suitor and "the other woman" as inadequate; moralistic literature must destroy or banish them before the final, happy resolution of the tale and the joining of the true partners. Lydia, who has swung between the extremes of self-indulgence and self-mortification throughout the novel, now considers suicide, but her recognition of "the depths of depravity" and her desire "to die, now" (321) are sufficient to remove her from the story as an active rival.

With Charlotte's only significant competitor now neutralized, the story can hurtle to its conclusion—the complete identification with and recognition of the true male figure demanded by the romance story, but achievable only through the heightened theatrics of an older form.

Melodrama has been described as a staged struggle between polar opposites, between higher and lower realms, heaven and hell, angels and demons. Throughout the novel, the anarchist Feliks has represented an alternative to the social order of Lord Walden's world and a sexual threat to his tidy domestic arrangements. In their competition for Charlotte, however, they become not so much opposites as the same—the *actants* of the knightly romance that Frederic Jameson argues are mirror images of each other.[20] The house is now on fire and both men rush side-by-side into the burning building in order to try to save the trapped Charlotte, and the novel describes them not so much as individuals anymore but as a unit: "They ran up the staircase. . . . They threw themselves at the door together," and so on (337). Yet important, dramatically crucial differences remain between the two characters.

Up until the moment of her screams, Feliks had persisted in denying love and in using Charlotte in his plans to assassinate the visiting Russian prince. When Charlotte recognizes his duplicity, and his denial of real love, Feliks is at long last revealed to her as the false father and her confusion is resolved.

The psychological divisions Freud writes of are akin to the divisions in allegory and in other didactic forms. The id/Bad Angel is at war with the superego/Good Angel for the destiny of the ego/Mankind.

Here, the pressures of the id, of Feliks who has led an animal-like existence for 19 years by foraging off the land, are shown as making one asocial, anarchistic: as a false attraction. Likewise, it is only when Walden becomes slightly less rigid and duty-bound, less dominated by the superego, that he can be revealed as the true father.

Bruno Bettleheim writes in *The Uses of Enchantment* (1977) that "integration of the disparate aspects of our personality can be gained only after the asocial, destructive, and unjust have been done away with,"[21] and this is precisely what happens within the burning manor at the end of *The Man from St. Petersburg:* unification of what the id can offer, but evaporation of the id's excess.

It is interesting how many Gothic romances—Gothic novels, for that matter, from Charlotte Brontë's *Jane Eyre* (1847) to Daphne Du Maurier's *Rebecca* (1938)—make use of a house, with all its enclosed rooms, as a kind of menacing presence. Rooms and interiors have often been seen as representing the sides of the personality and the fire as symbolically purging us of our more dangerous aspects. In the last scene, as flames start to engulf Charlotte, Walden takes "her entire weight," and the burden of being a genuine father, and tells her: "'All right, Papa's got you,'" thus reclaiming his rightful place. A kind of symbolic birthing process follows in which Walden draws "her through the hole" and out of the very room where sexual union with Feliks had been engaged in. The darker self can now be banished and destroyed: "As [Walden] pulled her out, the bedroom floor fell in, and Walden saw Feliks' face as Feliks dropped into the inferno" (339).

Traditional tales, and romance stories, often move from order through disturbance back to order, with the central characters fundamentally changed. Having confronted Feliks and what he represents, the divided Walden family can now be reunited. From the very end of the book:

Lydia looked at the fire burning down all those years of history, consuming the past. [Walden] came over and stood behind her. He whispered: "There was never anybody called Feliks." She looked up at him. Behind him, the sky in the east was pearly grey. Soon the sun would rise and it would be a new day. (340)

The triteness of the ending reinforces the melodramatic and fairy-tale quality, the working out of a girl's Oedipal conflicts. She can recognize her true parents only after they have become better people. And they have become better people only by understanding their darker selves and by recognizing that Charlotte has grown up.

In what one reviewer facetiously called "the most ill-advised epilogue in 20th-century literature," Follett moves directly from the climax and abandons falling action. Jane S. Bakerman has described this familiar Follett pattern from his middle novels as a way to "preserve history as we know it . . . [and] comfortingly suggest that worth merits happiness,"[22] a technique which results in the fable-like moral quality of the category romance. In this instance, the epilogue mentions not the death of the parents, but Charlotte's continued life, her finding of a life partner, and the validation of her political causes by her continued adherence to them, thus giving us the wish fulfillment common to the love story, to the melodrama, and to other traditional forms.

Follett, even in his later work, has remained interested in the category romance form and in applying those devices that appeal to female readers.

In 1990, for example, he published a short story entitled "The Abiding Heart," which, according to the advertising copy, was created "especially for *Good Housekeeping* [as] a compelling romance about an independent young woman who knows her own mind—until it comes to love."[23] In it, one finds all the formulaic ingredients of the "pure" romance story: the need to consider and discard a number of unsuitable alternatives, the use of a character foil and a strong third person point-of-view, the movement from order through disorder and back to harmony.

By then, however, Follett was already moving away from the strict category romance derivation and the classic espionage tale. With the publication of *The Pillars of the Earth* in 1989, he stepped more determinedly into the past and created a new blend: the historical thriller.

9

THE ARCHITECTURE OF THE NOVEL

The 19th-century German critic Gustav Freitag described the structural foundation of the well-made play and schematicized it as a five-part pyramid, with Exposition and Resolution as the twin corners of the base, Complication and Falling Action as the two sides, and the Crisis, of course, as the apex, or high point of the pyramid. It is doubtful that too many practicing authors today slavishly follow Freitag's geometrically precise diagram, but the comparison between building and writing remains an apt one, and is particularly appropriate in a discussion of Follett's 1989 bestseller *The Pillars of the Earth,* a work ironically enough about the building of a medieval cathedral.

This comparison suggests a certain projection of the writer into the work, necessary in all writing but particularly noticeable here. During the period of the book's construction, for example, Follett viewed himself as a craftsman (or "builder") rather than as an artist; he worked from an elaborate outline (or "blueprint") that took as long to write as the novel itself; and his stories can be considered carefully measured, fitted, even "built-up" through movable and re-usable descriptive blocks.

Architecture, therefore, becomes a central metaphor for the text and a way to understand Follett's working methods and the philosophy behind his art.

Follett has maintained that "[w]riting, particularly writing books that feature intrigue very heavily, is a process of calculating and plotting and twists and turns." On numerous occasions, Follett has shied from the label "artist" and has termed some of his critics "too high-minded." He once told *People* magazine: "I'm not under the illusion that the world is waiting for my thoughts to appear in print. . . . I think of myself as a craftsman more than an artist."[1] But the craft of writing—particularly of plot construction—is something that he has been especially conscious of and has worked into a number of his books.

In fact, the "blueprint," or outline, is central to his working methods: "I rewrite it many times," he stated in a 1986 interview, "trying to solve the problems at that stage." He then reworks that outline extensively with the input of an agent and editor and believes that, "when an outline is finished, the story is very clearly mapped out, so the process of writing the manuscript is almost a process of filling in the details."[2]

What differed in the construction process of *The Pillars of the Earth,* however, was the amount of time Follett spent establishing that foundation. Early in his career, Follett stated that "fast is my normal speed," and considered 3,000 publishable words in ten hours a good day. In fact, his best-known novel, the spy thriller *Eye of the Needle,* was the product of a mere three months' work. But the building of his 1,000-page chronicle of medieval life took over ten years' research time and an additional year and a half devoted to the outline alone.[3] Such a systematic composition method, however, may have resulted in a work which is indeed largely Freitagian, but also in a structure which is so immense that it overwhelms the characters and develops cracks of its own.

The story spans some 40 years and is set in the 12th century. Prior Phillip wants to build a successful monastery and later a cathedral at a time when two warring factions vie for the crown of England. A corrupt bishop and an ambitious earl plot to gain control of the new cathedral in order to advance their cause. Layered into this story of political machinations is the story of Tom, the builder, who marries Ellen, a mysterious woman from the woods, after his first wife has died in childbirth. An ancient family curse, famine, and warfare bring misfortune to the builders. The cathedral can only be completed when Prior Phillip outwits the ruthless bishop.

Follett has said that *The Pillars of the Earth* is not about religion but about inspiration, and allusions to faith were deliberately removed from an early title and book cover design. An avowed atheist, Follett has stated that "[t]he Church itself is not something I'm interested in," but in recounting the genesis of the novel, he explains how he was sent as a young reporter to East Anglia and "stood in awe of this incredible building, so high, so old, so beautiful," and he asked himself, "[w]hat drove them to build this?"[4]

As a possible outgrowth of his own feelings that "the medieval cathedrals of Europe . . . are technically brilliant and artistically breathtaking,"[5] the novel evenly balances good characters—those who are inspired to build—against the wicked characters determined to halt construction. On the one side are Prior Phillip, dedicated to building a successful organization and church; Tom, motivated by pride in construction; Ellen, devoted to rebuilding a family, and Aliena, a dispossessed noblewoman, who seeks to reconstruct her family fortune.

Set against them are the wicked earl, William, who wants to destroy the cathedral to extend his power base; the ambitious bishop, Waleran, who schemes rather than builds; Tom's complacent first wife Agnes, who wants money rather than inspiration from a cathedral; and the various henchmen who smash and pillage indiscriminately. Religious piety is also counterbalanced by ensuring that some of the good characters, such as Ellen, are religious skeptics and some of the bad characters, like William, are warped by religious zeal.

This careful positioning of opposing pillars is apparent in other ways as well:

Structurally, the novel is divided into five main parts with each of those parts about the length of one of Follett's previous spy novels (some 200+ pages). A 50-page coda (part vi) concludes the book.

In Hardyesque fashion, the novel begins with a hanging and ends with a hanging, traces the rising and falling fortunes of good and bad characters and the restoration of justice—at least poetic justice—through revenge.

Within the novel as a whole are a number of neatly divisible parallel scenes so that we have, for example, the evil Sheriff William's rape of his bride preceded by the good builder Jack's tender love scene. Through proximity alone (20 pages) these scenes comment on each other and link parts iv and v.

Builder Jack's designs, we are told, "were based on simple geometrical shapes" (772) so that proportion would become beautiful (527). "He drew a diamond, then a square inside a diamond, then a circle inside a square" (771). Within the novel itself, the groupings of opposing and linked characters have a similar neatness: in tandem with the idealistic Masterbuilder Jack, we find an equally inspired Prior Phillip, both dedicated to the cause of building the cathedral. And like chess pieces matched against them are Jack's brother Alfred, a shoddy builder and indifferent husband, and the ruthless Bishop Waleran, who connives for his own cathedral and lands.

This clear division and balancing and the author's obvious sympathy for those characters of vision raises the issue of projection, what a reviewer for *People Weekly* called "revelations of the novelist's alter-ego." Follett has said that a character of depth and conviction must in some way be an aspect of the writer's personality.[6] Physical descriptions and shared philosophies reinforce the idea that the novel serves as a vehicle for a discussion of how and why one should construct something. Prior Phillip, for example, is described as a short Welshman, who frowns frequently, and whose hair "was turning prematurely from black to gray" (465 and elsewhere). His creator has been described as "a dour Welshman" who "is short in stature and has graying black hair."[7] More importantly, perhaps, both were willing to engage in a work that "might take 15 years: one year for the foundations, four years for the chancel, four years for the transepts, and six years for the nave" (293).

The builders, of course, clearly function as replacements for the writer. Tom would make "many drawings, hundreds of them" and "would be drawing for years. But what he had in front of him was the essence of the building, and it was good: simple, inexpensive, graceful and perfectly proportioned" (290)—all structural goals of the popular writer. What motivates the writer generally is, as Tom states, "to create something from nothing" (291). These two central, sympathetic male characters—Prior Phillip and Builder Tom—serve, perhaps, as mouthpieces for the author's views: a common technique in fiction and film which tend toward the explicit expression of ideology.

The careful design of the novel is applied to the secondary characters, who are similarly balanced and aligned: The rightful Earl Richard is opposed by the usurper William, and the plucky, indomitable woman of the woods, Ellen, is paralleled by the plucky, indomitable noblewoman, Aliena. These extended stories are tied together through marriage or lust, so that Ellen is Jack's mother; Jack and Alfred are both in love with Aliena; and Richard, the displaced earl, is Aliena's brother.

As such, "family" becomes a central unifying mode in this chronicle, with the search for the parents a motivation for Jack (234, 918), the purging of a childhood sexual trauma an obsession for Richard and Phillip (888, 958), and the image of an "unholy" family—good people forced to live out of wedlock—used to connect two generations thematically. Not surprisingly, Jack acknowledges that in designing the cathedral "the task was much complicated by the religious significance of various numbers" (772) but a trinity does recur throughout the novel, as father, mother and child, three strong-willed women, three evil strangers, or three good versus three wicked men.

Tom, Jack's step-father:

designed the three levels of the nave wall—arcade, gallery and clerestory— strictly in the proportions 3:1:2. The arcade was half the height of the wall, the gallery was one third of the rest. Proportion was everything: it gave a subliminal feeling of rightness to the whole building. (289)

Substituting "writer" and "reader" for proper names in the next two sentences of this passage might give some sense of ways in which Follett may have projected "writerly" concerns into the text: "Studying the finished drawing, [the writer] thought it looked perfectly graceful. But would [the reader] think so?" (289).

Follett prefaced the advance galley of this book with a short note explaining that he has long been fascinated by Gothic cathedrals and has yearned to tell the story of how a single cathedral was erected. The amount of time spent planning this work attests to an abiding interest in the project. As we have indicated, the idea for *The Pillars of the Earth* began during his earliest professional writing days when, as a journalist for the London *Evening News,* he was assigned to cover a story in East Anglia and visited a 12th-century cathedral. Some two years later, in 1976, he produced an initial draft of a novel about the building of a medieval cathedral but abandoned it because "I didn't know enough about cathedrals then; I didn't even know enough about novels."[8] Over the next ten years, Follett immersed himself in medieval history, spent weekends visiting cathedrals throughout England, and in 1986 was again ready to undertake the all-important outline.

But despite the careful planning and the almost Walter Scott-like symmetry of the work, reviewer Cecilia Holland felt that the story was like "a cathedral built too high," one that "develops cracks and chunks of it fall into the crypt." Perhaps it was the size and scale of the project itself—a story which would include historical melodrama[9] covering four generations, the collapse and rebuilding of a medieval cathedral, an English civil war, a pilgrimage to Spain, the murder of Thomas à Becket, and a multitude of other violent and dramatic incidents—that would create too much stress for the design; a parallel problem which Builder Jack considers when cracks appear in *his* cathedral built too high: "[He] had not found a solution to the problem. . . . There was something crucially wrong with his design. The structure was strong enough to support the weight of the vault, but not to resist the winds that blew so hard against the high walls" (871).

Other reviewers noted similar fault lines: Richard Novak remarked that "toward the end, Follett starts throwing in frequent recaps of the story's highlights, as if he thought that the book needed a little padding," and Cynthia Johnson, writing for *Library Journal,* termed the plot "less tightly controlled than those in Follett's contemporary works."[10]

But there are a number of ways in which the novel is solidly constructed, or at the very least is clearly "built by" Follett: in his blending of generic sources, in the transference of movable scenes, and in his use of descriptive blocks—the most problematic of the three techniques.

His first building technique, however—the interlocking of formulaic features from one category with those of another—has always been a principal strength in his writing because it has allowed him to create slightly new forms. This was certainly the case with his first published novel, *The Big Needle* (1974), which merged a British writing style with the American hard-boiled genre, and with his runaway success four years later, *Eye of the Needle,* which integrated espionage and love story elements, thus appealing to a wider audience. So too, in *The Pillars of the Earth,* Follett was able to blend materials from antecedent literary sources (*The Canterbury Tales, Ivanhoe,* and *Robin Hood,* above all) with those from more contemporary works, including his own numerous mystery and suspense novels.

From Chaucer we find an interest in the make-up of society itself, with its representative figures "the knight, the monk and the priest" (15) and the journey/pilgrimage motif, here to Compostela and Tours. From Sir Walter Scott we find the lavish battle scene descriptions, both panoramic and close-up, the carefully matched characters and the interest in melodrama and popular forms. I suppose it is impossible for any popular English writer, whether Buchan or Follett, to think of the 12th century without thinking of *Ivanhoe* (1819). Buchan found much to admire in Scott's writing and if Follett, who has sometimes employed a more American writing style to appeal to an American audience, draws materials from Sir Walter Scott, it is a return to an "Englishness" that is not found in all of his international bestsellers. In the same way that the Western functions as an enduring and renewable mythos in American popular culture, the Medieval Romance, whether Malory's *Morte d'Arthur,* Scott's *Ivanhoe,* or *The Legend of Robin Hood,* serves in a similar fashion to provide a kind of cultural identity or outlook in England, especially for young persons, "the most common readers of romance."[11] In fact, both *Ivanhoe* and *Robin Hood* were popular British television shows when Follett was a schoolboy and when *Gunsmoke* and *Rawhide* ruled America's airwaves.

Consequently, one finds clear comparisons between Follett's *The Pillars of the Earth* and *The Legend of Robin Hood.* Not only is *Pillars* in part a story of the dispossessed, with Ellen and her band hiding in the forest and the honest Prior Phillip a kind of Friar Tuck, but it is the saga of the rightful Earl Richard's struggle against the wicked Earl William, reminiscent of the struggle between Richard the Lionhearted and King John. In Follett's medieval romance, however, *his* Richard heads off to the Holy Land rather than returning from it and his wicked lord is both sheriff and earl, a combined King John and Sheriff of Nottingham.

Elements from the spy melodrama and from Follett's other works are liberally mixed-in, creating an amalgam which Patrick Reardon of the *Chicago Tribune* suggested is a new form, the "historical thriller," since Follett had "successfully adapted his thriller-writing skills to the task of historical fiction."[12] In fact, this becomes his second most important building technique—the transference of entire scenes from one genre or one novel to another—since it allows him to place in *The Pillars of the Earth* such classic espionage moments as the ordinary man who discovers a secret that determines the fate of nations (107) and the search for the parent or father-figure (918), as well as his own suspense scenes practiced and perfected in his other books: the knife fight (57) from *The Key to Rebecca;* the burning building (234) from *The Man from St. Petersburg;* the spunky tom-boy (35) from *Lie Down with Lions;* even some of the sexual fetishes (70) from *Lie Down with Lions* and other works. Each time, there is sufficient variation upon a set scene for the familiar to seem new.

But a third technique—the replication of descriptive phrases—especially when occurring within the same novel, seems less an effective building method than it does a routine borrowing. From three very different stages of Follett's writing career we find three very similar chapter openings: "It was the coldest winter for forty-five years" (*Needle* 3); "It was going to be a hot day;"[13] and "[t]he winter came early and it was as cold and hard and unyielding as a stonemason's chisel" (*Pillars* 58)—each attention-getter reliant on a simple and dramatic statement of extreme weather conditions and using an "it was" expletive construction.

At times, the physical descriptions of individuals are similarly interchangeable. In *Eye of the Needle,* the German spy, Faber, "was a fine figure of a man: tall, quite heavy around the shoulders, not a bit fat, with long legs" (6). William, in *The Pillars of the Earth,* is equally Teutonic: "The young lord was a tall, well-built fellow of about twenty years, with yellow hair and narrow eyes which made him look as if he were always peering into the sun" (25). And when such linguistic repetitions recur within the same novel, the effect is a lull in the novel's progress. Within a few pages of *The Pillars of the Earth,* Tom finds "the road falling away gently before them in a long curve" (41) and then sees "the Winchester road, going east, dead straight, like a long carpet unrolled over the hills" (53). In traveling to Salisbury, Tom's family "crested a rise" (41)—a verbal expression used for Phillip's similar experience when he too "crested the next rise" (121). Additionally, throughout the novel Prior Phillip is identified by a nearly exact descriptive phraseology; by his "graying hair" (801) and "worried frown" (291), a labeling technique which may be convenient, especially in a long novel, but which also fixes characters and curtails further growth.

A lack of psychological development in characters was a criticism leveled against Sir Walter Scott by Georg Lukács who held that the author of an historical novel must maintain the same artistic conventions of portrayal and style as any other novelist. Yet in the case of a popular writer such as Follett, especially one who does not consider the term "popular" to be a pejorative,[14] this approach of methodically "filling in the details" may well represent a competing philosophy of artistic construction. In fact, a belief in the solid positioning of parts is shared by Builder Tom who "directs workers to stack stones in an interlocking pattern so that the pile would not topple" (258) and is also expressed by Tom's step-son, Jack, who believes that "the stones had to fit together precisely, otherwise the carvings would not line up and the illusion would be spoiled" (557).

Another popular historical novelist, Rhona Martin, also places a great emphasis on the soundness of design, maintaining that "constructing the novel is undoubtedly one of the most difficult aspects of writing, where many otherwise promising writers lose their way. . . . Good construction will ensure that there are no loose ends straggling off into the distance" and must all be done "without anyone noticing it at work." These precepts indicate that for many popular writers it is not character, or theme, or setting, or literary style which predominates, but plot—a feature remarked on by Janice Radway in her study of the category romance. For the mass readership of that genre, "well-written" tends to mean an ingenious plot.[15]

Nevertheless, in *The Pillars of the Earth,* it is perhaps this very insistence on the mechanical construction of the book, on its architecture, that resulted in two overarching problems: in a stasis for the characters, what Cecilia Holland called a lack of "some deepening emotional discovery,"[16] and in a general bulkiness.

As indicated earlier, the use of descriptive building blocks and identification tags such as "the frown," "the missing ear," or "the stoop," not only sets characters physically but to a large extent emotionally as well. An archetypal character such as William, for example, indulges the single emotion of hatred for 35 years and Richard is driven by a grievance for about as long. Clearly, Follett is working in a hybrid form, and while it is true that the revenge saga appropriately makes use of one-dimensional stock figures—the wicked nobleman, the cunning cleric, the maiden in distress—characters that may be driven by single and simple emotions, it is also true that the modern novel demands some sort of character growth, "epiphany" or moment of illumination.

Second, with his stated "need to take a break from [writing thrillers],"[17] Follett turned to an older form—the historical novel—and to an older structural design—the Freitagian pyramid. With its six book-length divisions, this 1,000-page saga makes use of a number of individual and historical crises for dramatic tension. But one particular high point of action—the collapse of Winchester Cathedral—represents a defining moment for all the key characters, since they will subsequently endeavor either to rebuild the cathedral or to prevent its being rebuilt.

In the same way that Margaret Mitchell had placed the "Burning of Atlanta" near the center of her historical novel, Follett has positioned his visually and thematically important disaster in the middle of part iv, relatively close to the exact center of *The Pillars of the Earth*. But if the outcome is a strictly Freitagian pyramid, it is one without the complicated and appealing characters of a Rhett Butler or a Scarlett O'Hara needed to carry readers down the pyramid's long second side called Falling Action.

Moreover, as a number of contemporary writers have recognized, Freitag's 19th-century schema for the construction of the well-made play ignored the actual reality of most play construction. As fiction writer Janet Burroway points out, Frietag's diagram:

visually suggests that a crisis comes in the middle of the "pyramid" shape of a plot, whereas even in a five act drama the crisis is usually saved for the middle of the fifth act; and in modern fiction, particularly the compact short-story form, the falling action is likely to be brief or non-existent.[18]

Much of Follett's popular work has made use of this more contemporary pattern, which in part accounts for the success of his various spy thrillers. In *Twentieth-Century Crime and Mystery Writers,* Jane S. Bakerman notes that a Follett thriller begins near the moment of crisis, then fills in the background of characters while moving relentlessly toward the climax, where action breaks off abruptly. In so doing, "Follett avoids anti-climactic denouement by simply abandoning falling action; instead, he appends final details in an epilogue." Bakerman maintains that this non-Freitagian pattern works particularly well in novels about recent history since we already know the ultimate outcome of the adventure: "[T]he heroes have achieved their goals—they have preserved history as we know it; they have defended a just cause; and they have demonstrated that one person can make a difference."[19]

By abandoning a successful contemporary formula and by patterning *The Pillars of the Earth* on an older, Freitagian design, Follett built up a multi-storied structure with the same problems of stress as faced by his medieval architect: how to create ever larger and longer forms successfully. In the important historical shift from the plain Norman church style to the excesses of Gothic cathedrals, medieval builders solved *their* problem of structural stress by adding on more and more visible, external support struts. Follett's own move from the purity of the thriller form to the massiveness of the historical novel has resulted in a work with the flying buttresses equally exposed—five long sections, a 50-page addendum and the Crisis closer to the apex of the pyramid. The aesthetic objection to Gothic cathedrals has always been that they were essentially enlarged Norman churches with the builder's scaffolding still attached.

Follett has been someone who has reacted to changes within his own time as well as someone who has acted to initiate change. Realizing that a novel about the Middle Ages would not be marketable in the 1970s, he waited until after Umberto Eco's *The Name of the Rose* was published in 1983 before he returned to the subject of a medieval cathedral.[20] *The Pillars of the Earth* came out in 1989, the same year that the Berlin wall was breached, and for popular writers of Follett's generation, the end of the Cold War marked both the end of East-West hostilities as well as the end of the lucrative spy genre.

The Pillars of the Earth also represents the first of Follett's "Robin Hood" novels and the furthering of the "rich versus poor" theme he had touched on in *The Man from St. Petersburg.* His next three novels—*A Dangerous Fortune* (1993), *A Place Called Freedom* (1995), and *The Third Twin* (1996) would all expand on the theme of social inequity, with two of the novels making use of an historical setting.

By turning to history, Follett could find a new literary territory as well as a landscape for his alter-ego characters. "I think you can only write about another historical period," Follett said in late 1989, "on the assumption that people in that period are basically the same as people today. Otherwise the readers wouldn't identify with the characters in the story."[21]

Through the revision and recasting of history, Follett increasingly would find a more appropriate vehicle than the Cold War novel for the expression and projection of a contemporary political ideology.

10

POLITICS AND HISTORICAL REVISIONISM

In this next to the last chapter, we will discuss the politics and religion that have underlain Follett's novels from the very beginning.

As early as 1979, Follett recognized that the "literary phenomenon of the decade is the romantic-historical blockbuster—the kind of book my English agent calls a Sweet Savage Hysterical,"[1] but found himself discouraged from writing one. His novels up until that point had all been contemporary hard-boiled detective stories and tales of industrial espionage—fiction that would appeal primarily to a male and probably conservative readership—and, of course, his World War II thriller *Eye of the Needle,* set in the not-too-distant past.

Perhaps because "historical" would have implied "political" as well, Follett suppressed his own Labour Party views and produced a runaway bestseller with an Oxford don as its hero, the War Office in Whitehall as its locus, and Winston Churchill in a fond cameo. Before writing the book which was to establish his international success, Follett was warned by his American agent, Al Zuckerman, that "the American book-buyer is not interested in the details of English working-class life. People do not want to buy a book that tells them about the grim humdrum lives of ordinary people." Instead, he wrote a book which earned him financial independence and which continues to sell at the rate of some 50,000 copies per year.[2] *Triple,* his next book, was published the same year that Margaret Thatcher became prime minister, in 1979. Ronald Reagan was inaugurated as president some two years later, and throughout the 1980s Follett's war-time and Cold War thrillers enjoyed a vast readership in a largely conservative United States. During that period of time, the appeal of conservative political leaders was partially the same as the appeal of espionage novels: both played on the fears, even the paranoia of an audience, that anything less than fervent nationalism would be seen as a weakness.

Ironically, Follett's financial freedom to turn toward historical fiction and to express Labour Party views was earned through sales to a conservative following. Both Britain and the United States have changed in electoral attitudes since the 1980s, and the populism expressed in his two most recent historical novels, *A Dangerous Fortune* (1993) and *A*

Place Called Freedom (1995), find resonance in part because the readership has changed.

With the end of the Cold War, the old domestic ghosts of social class in Britain, racial and regional politics in the United States, and the social and political role of women in both countries, have returned as central issues, ones that an electorate have generally viewed as better addressed by liberal politicians. Neil Kinnock's Labour Party gained significant majorities in several important municipal councils by the end of the 1980s and had been expected to win the general election of 1992. That same year, Bill Clinton was elected president and four years later became the first Democratic president in almost half a century to receive a second term.

This change in political attitudes has perhaps been another reason for Follett's willingness to write more decidedly ideological fiction. Concerned about alienating half his readers if he were to write on modern politics, he has stated that the advantage to writing historical novels is that "everybody's pretty much in agreement who are the good guys and who are the bad guys. [The] political arguments have pretty much been settled."[3] As we shall see, however, the unsettled political arguments of today are the ones Follett is most interested in projecting onto the past. His selective vision of the Georgian and Victorian eras has resulted in a reworking of history, and yet in two works which are perhaps stronger as fiction than many of his other books because of that very inclusion of a contemporary political ideology.

These two books were the end product of the much criticized "Dell Deal." In 1990, Dell Publishing Company announced that it would pay Follett $12.3 million for two books which he had not yet written. The discrepancy between his personal wealth and his socialist outlook has raised some criticism in the British press, but Follett has defended both the Dell Deal as well as his more recent political activities, arguing that it's "an old-fashioned definition of socialism" to say only the poor and working class should be involved. "If you believe in '*from* each according to his ability, *to* each according to his need,' then the people who've got the money should give it [to the Labour Party]."[4]

Follett's second wife, the former Barbara Broer, has also been asked to discuss the surface incompatibility between personal fortune and Marxist-Socialist thought. She has explained that when she married Follett in 1985, she "found the fact that he was rich . . . a little unnerving." An activist in liberal politics, she has stated that even though being rich "is very pleasant, if you've spent your life identifying the rich as the enemy, you become the enemy. But that has resolved itself now. It's what you use the money for that matters."[5]

At the time, Barbara Follett was an image consultant for the Labour Party and, given her experiences in South Africa where she had lived for many years, more publicly political than her husband was. In a separate interview with Lesley White, she explained that "I have dragged Ken further into Labour Politics than he was before I met him. I have certainly helped spend his money on it." In 1988, he established a scholarship in the memory of her slain husband, Richard Turner, a South African civil rights activist, and pledged to fund the scholarship "until South Africa is free." He underwrote the first Labour $800-a-plate dinner in 1991, organized another fund-raising dinner in 1994 and hosted a $48,000 birthday party to which Neil Kinnock, then Labour Party leader, was invited. Accused of running a fashionable salon in his $3.2 million home in London's Chelsea neighborhood, Follett has stated that the monthly events are not "consciously political occasions. . . . But yes, those guests . . . they're all Lefties, aren't they?"[6]

He held the formal position of press officer and later celebrity unit chair for the Labour Party, a position from which he resigned in 1995. "I would quite like to write a novel with a great political message," he stated that same year, "like *The Grapes of Wrath* or *To Kill a Mockingbird* or even *Oliver Twist*. But . . . I probably am just not angry enough."[7] He has stayed active in behind-the-scenes political events, however, and helped his wife win election to Parliament in 1997 as part of the landslide Labour victory led by Tony Blair.

Although he credits his wife with pulling him back into the Labour Party,[8] Follett's own religious and social background were as important in the formation of those political sensibilities and convictions which infuse *A Dangerous Fortune* and *A Place Called Freedom* as were any more recent events.

In fact, Follett's personal and political maturation roughly parallels the development of the British Labour Party in the post-war period. Born three years after the general election of 1946, Follett was raised in a lower-middle-class neighborhood during the time of Clement Atlee's "Quiet Revolution" and in a region—Wales—that had long been dominated by the Labour party.

The general election of 1946, of course, represented Labour's return to power after a generation, the beginning of the modern welfare state, and the nationalization of various industries.

Follett notes that "the Britain I grew up in was a society completely formed by socialist ideas. We had free health care, I was paid a wage to go to college, millions of people lived in well-built government housing, and everyone had the vote; and still enterprising people could become millionaires."[9]

Moreover, in a country where the nonconformist religions have often been associated with dissent, Follett's parents were devout members of the Plymouth Brethren sect. He remembers attending church three times each Sunday and once or twice each weekday evening until he was old enough to leave home. We have discussed the influence of the Bible on his literary style, but religion can be the foundation for political ideas as well. In addition to the anti-establishment stance historically of much British Protestantism, the reformist instincts of Christian-Humanism generally have often been seen as a precursor to Marxist-Socialist thought. Erich Fromm describes Marxism as "a protest imbued with faith in man, in his capacity to liberate himself, and to realize his potentialities" and has demonstrated the Old Testament roots in Marx's world view, calling it "essentially prophetic Messianism in the language of the nineteenth century."[10]

Follett, as well, has noted this connection, explaining that [t]he move from fundamentalist religion to socialism is a common one,"[11] and the ties between Christian-Humanism and Marxist-Socialism are clearly shown in the Labour Party doctrine of his childhood. In the 1950s, Labour held that since society is divided unfairly into classes whose interests conflict, a leveling in society is needed to bring about justice. Only through programmatic policies will this equality be achieved.

In the late 1960s, two additional developments took place within the Labour Party: a number of the Trade Unions, and their voters, came under the control of leaders with Marxist sympathies; and the "New Left" movement, headed by students who were opposed to the American involvement in Viet Nam, came into being. These two groups dominated the British Labour Party during this period and gave it a more radical stamp.

This was also the time of Follett's undergraduate studies at University College, London. Entering in 1967, he undertook a degree in Philosophy. "Given my religious background," he has stated, "it was a natural thing to do." But by the following year—the year of the Paris student strikes—he had renounced the religion of his childhood and was leading a student protest against the University exam system. As he has described it, "[t]he great thing about nonconformist religions is that they are argumentative. So they give you the tools with which to reject them. But you are left feeling that life should be guided by a profound principle, and you search for a more rational one."[12]

Having received his degree and as a beginning journalist and novelist working in two very conservative areas—the tabloid press and mass-market paperbacks—Follett played only a minor role in the Labour Party during the time when it was controlled by the extreme Left. After

Labour's crushing defeat in the 1987 general election, Neil Kinnock declared that the party would have to moderate its policies if it had any hope of winning on the national level. The Labour Party then began to court centrists and successful entrepreneurs, among them Follett, who by the 1980s had also tempered his views.[13] These more business-oriented members have been called "New Labour."

As we have seen, the late 1980s marked Follett's acceptance of a prominent role in Labour Party affairs—and his return to a religious subject in *The Pillars of the Earth,* a subject now dampened by his declared atheism: "What does interest me is [not the Church but] the struggle to create a more decent society, a more civilized world. At that moment in history, the Church served that function."[14] Clearly, Follett feels that the Labour Party serves that function today and he has incorporated those views into his two most recently published historical novels, even at the risk of alienating his former readers. Through a recognition of the roots of Marxist-Socialism, however, he may have carried those readers with him.

Both *A Dangerous Fortune* and *A Place Called Freedom* can be read as political novels, ones in which the characters "think in terms of supporting or opposing society as such."[15] More importantly, they exhibit specific Marxist-Socialist ideas by focusing on periods when the struggle between labor and capital was acute, by emphasizing the opposition of the haves and the have nots, and by arguing that those who do not embrace the class struggle are the worst people of all.

A Dangerous Fortune, Follett's novel about a banking dynasty, is set in late-19th-century Britain at a time of largely unrestrained bond trading and of huge disparities in wealth. Two sets of characters are linked through the secret of a drowning death at an exclusive boys' school: Edward Pilaster, the vicious heir to a banking fortune, and his equally wealthy and corrupt South American friend, Micky Miranda; aligned against them are Hugh Pilaster, Edward's hard-working but impoverished cousin, and Tonio Silva, also from South America but from a less influential family.

The novel follows their adult paths and describes a complex power struggle and loan scheme. Allied with Edward is his low-born mother, Augusta, a cunning and manipulative woman who yearns for a title. Helping Hugh is a Jewish prostitute, Maisie, whose laboring family was ruined by a bank failure and who later selflessly opens a shelter for destitute women. As reviewer Kate Saunders noted, Follett's characters in *A Dangerous Fortune* "are blackest black, or whitest white, without a single shade of grey" and serve to "make speeches about the bloody bosses, and debate the morality of banking as a profession."[16]

Similarly didactic in arrangement and storyline is Follett's 1995 novel about indentured servants and Scottish coal miners who were slaves. Set in the late 18th century when landlords and shippers sometimes literally owned their workers, *A Place Called Freedom* pits Mack McAsh, a defiant miner, against Jay Jamisson, the younger son of a Scottish mine-owning family. Equally defiant and independent-minded is Lizzie Hallam, who is attracted to Mack and wants to help him, even though she is a member of the gentry (but from an impoverished family). Mack escapes the mines only to find work as a coal-heaver in London where another brutal system of exploitation exists, held in place by former workers who have become middle-men.

Eventually, Lizzie is forced to marry Jay and the two immigrate to Virginia to establish a tobacco plantation. Mack, who has tried to lead a workman's strike, is deported to America as an indentured servant and ends up on the Jamisson's land. "The characters are stereotypes," Patricia Altner observed in writing for *Library Journal,* "and coincidental meetings abound, but the historical picture of suffering and injustice done to the poor is well drawn."[17]

Clearly, the pattern of plot and the intersecting lives of good and bad characters allow for sharp contrasts, but Follett develops the dialectic in other ways as well—through the use of admirable characters who serve as mouthpieces for favored ideas, villainous characters who represent the opposing view, authorial irony which verges on satire, and scenes designed to elicit emotions of great pity.

In the first place, readers normally sympathize with characters who have suffered unfairly, and Follett ensures that a critique of the banking system in *A Dangerous Fortune* is spoken by a man who has lost his fortune twice. "The men who own the banks are the stupidest people in the world," he says. "They never learn, so they make the same mistakes again and again. And it's the workingmen who suffer" (210). In *A Place Called Freedom,* Follett makes certain that the outcry against overcharging coal-heavers is spoken by a man who has been doubly wronged: as a worker and as "an English Negro with a flat Newcastle accent" who is still an honest man (152). In Marxist fashion, the book also emphasizes the workers' solidarity that should cut across regional or racial divisions in this and in later scenes where exploited whites and blacks mix in easy familiarity.

In both books, Follett allows sympathetic central characters to express political views close to his own, or uses irony of situation to deride representatives of the opposing view. As a Leftist, Follett believes in the leveling of society and the doing away of class privilege. He has said that "there is this group that is distinguished only because it is distinguished, at the apogee of which is the royal family. They are the most boring people in London. . . . the least interesting group you could possibly hang out with."[18] In *A Dangerous Fortune,* Follett has the kindly Uncle Seth express parallel views when he exclaims that he disapproves of the royal family because he "disapprove[s] of idleness" (40), and in a later scene has the heroic Hugh Pilaster encounter a brothel madam dressed up like Queen Victoria and observe that "[s]he acts like royalty!" (86).

These techniques of sympathetic identification with one point-of-view and the deflation through irony of the other are used in *A Place Called Freedom* as well. Mack McAsh, the brutalized, long-suffering hero, speculates that "sheer conservatism had led [the ship owners] to side with people they knew, regardless of justice" (203), and in a facetious allusion to a rival novelist, the Tory peer Jeffrey Archer, Follett makes certain that many of the scenes of upper-class decadence take place in "Lord Archer's Coffeehouse."

His second technique of placing disfavored political opinions in the mouths of less-than-savory characters is another well-honed device from ideological fiction, and in Marxist-Socialist manner these villains tend to be "class traitors," people who, like Margaret Thatcher and like Aunt Augusta in *A Dangerous Fortune,* had started out "nothing special. Her father was a shop assistant who had started his own business and ended up with three little grocery stores in the west London suburbs" but who believe themselves "clearly destined for higher things" (*DF* 201).

Not only have such people apparently turned their backs on lower-middle-class origins similar to his own, but they have risen by embracing the values of their natural class enemies. They themselves become, as Follett has the sympathetic character Maisie state in *A Dangerous Fortune,* "the snobs and shrews who ruled society" (342).

His comments on the actual Margaret Thatcher are no-less-direct. "I don't admire her in any way at all," he has said. "She's brutal, cruel and has a puny intellect,"[19] and where these two novels use the third technique of authorial irony bordering on satire is in depicting the pretensions of such social climbers: Augusta, in *A Dangerous Fortune,* is aghast at the thought that "[t]here were no rules anymore! Anyone could enter society" (489), and Jay Jamisson, the son of a wealthy merchant in *A Place Called Freedom,* is "infuriated . . . to see people getting above their station. . . . In the colonies, now, a slave was a slave, and no nonsense about working a year and a day or being paid wages. That was the way to do things, in Jay's opinion" (25). In both instances, whatever value the statements might have is undercut by the treatment. The superfluous exclamation point and the unqualified generalization "anyone" make Aunt Augusta seem alarmist; so too, the unnecessary asides "now" and "in Jay's opinion" turn his observations into self-important pronouncements.

A fourth technique is the use of direct commentary to guide readers' sympathies within clearly delineated scenes, as when Follett points to "the squat hovels . . . [that] made people think of Hell" (*DF* 62) and to the stately homes of the rich which have kitchens "the size of a small church" (*DF* 170). When such visual contrasts are perhaps not enough, the writer will lead us even more completely as when we are told that frosty mornings were "delightful if you had a fur coat, torture if you lived in a drafty slum" (*DF* 258).

Certainly such contrasts existed between the "Two Englands," as Thomas Hines and others have pointed out, but the highly selective vision, the camera that focuses exclusively on the poor and the rich, on a Marxist dialectic, ignores other kinds of realities about the Georgian or Victorian worlds. For example, the 18th-century movement to abolish the slave trade was led by a member of the landed gentry and of Parliament, William Wilberforce, and the term the "Two Englands" comes from an early social protest novel written, in fact, by Queen Victoria's prime minister, Benjamin Disraeli.[20] Both eras were marked not only by smugness and complacency but also by serious considerations regarding the nature of wealth, the consequences of industrialization, and the obligations of the society toward the less fortunate.

In essence, these techniques of the highly selective view, the manipulation of characters and statements, and the contrivance of scenes are the standard devices of the committed ideologue and pamphleteer. Sheer propaganda is usually off-putting for even a general audience, yet Follett designed the two books in part to win new readers. Clearly, other factors are at work, too; if satire and stereotyping are part of political campaigns, they are inherent in Follett's chosen literary form as well—melodrama.

A number of reviewers have commented on the connection between stereotypes and entertainment in his well-told tales. Chris Petrakos, in a review of *A Place Called Freedom,* pointed out that "while we've seen many of these characters before . . . this is [still] a very entertaining tale." The critic for *Publishers' Weekly* argued that "Follett's characters [in *A Dangerous Fortune*] are drawn with broad, realistic strokes, and his skill at plotting and taste for sexual intrigue keep the melodrama moving in high gear."[21] In a sense, the inclusion of stock characters accounts for the novels' readability, and the reduction of moral complexity for their vast appeal.

Melodrama requires easily recognizable characters whose vices or virtues are clear, and 19th-century melodrama often held up portrayals of heroes or heroines that were flattering to a large audience. In line with both Labour Party thinking and American bookbuying habits, Follett's sympathetic characters are progressive women, resilient workers, and the rich who are self-made.

Follett has stated on several occasions that many of his readers are female. In both *A Dangerous Fortune* and *A Place Called Freedom,* we find forward-looking and largely anachronistic women characters whose sexual or political assertiveness is expressed in contemporary terms. Lizzie Hallam, for example, refers to Mack McAsh as "good enough to eat" (125), and Maisie Robinson, in *A Dangerous Fortune,* considers what she would do if "some self-righteous Conservative got up in Parliament and said that most unmarried women were prostitutes . . . , or some such rot" (434). These sorts of comments prompted one reviewer for *Publishers' Weekly* to observe that Follett is keeping his contemporary, and probably largely female, readership firmly in mind.[22]

Equally comforting for suburban book-buyers is the favorable image of the lower-middle class and of those who have improved themselves through dint of effort.

American and British workers often consider their strengths to be frankness, good humor and a lack of inhibitions. In *A Dangerous Fortune,* Hugh Pilaster must find a kind of moral redemption by entering that sanctum of the British working class: the music hall. Here, he can sing "at the top of his voice. He was feeling good. He had eaten a pint of winkles and drunk several glasses of warm, malty beer" (298). What in other books might be viewed as "slumming" is here seen as an escape from the artificiality of his class. In addition, Hugh, who has been kept from his rightful place in the bank because of his Aunt's scheming, eventually gains control through sheer talent and hard work.

While Mack MacAsh, in *A Place Called Freedom,* may not eat winkles, jellied eels especially enjoyed by the poor, positive stereotypes abound, from his workman's dignity in refusing "to scramble for the wages he had earned" (150) to his vital sexuality: "half naked . . . , the massive muscles of his back bunched and rolled as he swung his hammer" (66)—a formula ingredient from many kinds of melodrama where the hero must be low-born but handsome. Mack, too, who for so long had been a servant or a slave, finally owns his own farm in large part because of his diligence.

The rewarding of the good and the just, the punishment of the wicked are key patterns in 19th-century moralistic plays and novels, as is the use of sentiment. Harriet Beecher Stowe is noted for her emotive treatment of the very poor. This sentimentality takes two forms: seeing individuals as a unit, all of whom are deserving of pity, as in a passage from *Uncle Tom's Cabin:*

Slowly the weary, dispirited creatures wound their way into the room, and with crouching reluctance, presented their baskets to be weighed.[23]

—or in a section from *A Place Called Freedom:*

The coal heavers' wives began to appear, many of them with babies in their arms and children clinging to their skirts. Some had the spirit and beauty of youth, but others looked weary and underfed, the beaten wives of violent and drunken men. (149)

—and second, lingering on certain extreme emotions such as loss, grief, loneliness, despair, etc. Stowe writes:

There was a small book, which had been given to her by Eva, containing a single verse of Scripture, arranged for every day in the year, and in a paper the curl of hair that she had given her on that memorable day when she had taken her last farewell. (444)

The sentiment is in part derived by the isolation of an object that represents the dead Eva and by the use of reductive modifiers: "small," "single," "last." Follett writes in similar fashion when he describes Maisie's narrow surroundings in *A Dangerous Fortune:*

There was only one picture on the wall. . . . It was her only souvenir of those days. Otherwise the room contained only a narrow bed, a washstand, one chair and a three-legged stool. . . . The dirt on the window served instead of curtains. (204)

Here, a picture rather than a book becomes the reminder of those by-gone days to be dwelt upon, and the modifiers "one" or "only" are used to evoke an excess of emotion.

In both *A Dangerous Fortune* and *A Place Called Freedom,* not only are the very poor treated sentimentally—a feature of melodrama—but the rich must make contact with the poor in order to be redeemed. Women characters who come of age sexually, and to some extent politically, have inhabited Follett's novels at least since *The Man From St. Petersburg* (1982). If, in his earlier works, the emphasis was on their sexual awakening and on their understanding of the world as an evil place, the emphasis is now on privileged individuals, male and female both, who grow primarily in political awareness: Hugh, in *A Dangerous Fortune,* is "mortified to think his own family and their bank were financing such a brutal industry" (325) and Lizzie, in *A Place Called Freedom,* is amazed to find that the miners' "lives were brutally hard

[but] their spirits seemed unquenchable. By comparison her own life seemed pampered and purposeless" (69). The stories are now as much about right and wrong as they are about good and evil, and the development of a social conscience gives to the characters a moral complexity and the necessary "deepening emotional discovery"[24] which Cecilia Holland found lacking in an earlier historical novel and which now add gradations to the stock figures.

In the preface to his 1957 study on *Politics and the Novel,* Irving Howe maintained that the political novel "must contain the usual representation of human behavior and feeling; yet it must also absorb into its stream of movement the hard and perhaps insoluble pellets of modern ideology" (20). By including these grains of contemporary political outlook in a novel about the past, Follett is better able to achieve that concrete representation of human emotion: his characters are passionate about change in an almost religious way. At times, of course, those attitudes seem out-of-place in novels about the 18th or 19th centuries, as when Aunt Augusta decides that "the bad temper of middle-aged men had to do with the amount of meat they ate" (*DF* 356) or when the author observes that the aristocracy "would stay in the country, slaughtering birds, hunting foxes. . . . [and] idly persecuting dumb animals in the countryside" (*DF* 122), giving to the novels what one reviewer calls "the faint aura of political correctness."[25]

And despite his demurrers on the absence of religion in his thinking, Follett's 18 years of Plymouth Brethren upbringing are projected onto several of the characters in these two books, giving them a complex set of moral values, tempered at times by Marxism, that moves them well beyond stereotype. The bank, for example, is described as a temple of evil where the "moneylenders . . . acted as if charging interest were a noble calling, like the priesthood" (*DF* 193) and the Scottish miners sing a religious hymn about "that heavenly city [where] all men shall be free" (97) when they first defy the owners. In a sense, both books trace the beginnings of trade unionism in Britain and show that the initial "feeling of fellowship and triumph" (*PC* 22) in church are later transformed into similar emotions of solidarity amongst "the thousands of working people [thrown] into destitution" (*DF* 264).

Other parallels to his own life come through in his attitude toward those who have moved-up in society through their own efforts (*DF* 255) but who have not forgotten their origins (*PC* 159) and in his sometimes ambivalent attitude toward material wealth. Follett may have been an affiliated member of the Labour Party since leaving college, but he has not always been Labour's symbol "of affluent altruism . . . [and] totem of [Neil] Kinnock's brave new middle-class." In 1983, while living in an

Edwardian country home staffed by five servants—three for the house and two for the garden—Follett remarked that "[o]f all the things I have that could be bought with money, the house is what gives me the most pleasure. . . . Other than that, well, I do spend an inordinate amount of money on clothes. It's almost a vice. I have a wine cellar, which is the nearest thing I have to a hobby. I go to auctions and buy vintage Bordeaux wines and drink them. I buy young wines and keep them."[26]

In the novels, that same ambivalent attitude toward wealth—that it's "wonderful not to have to ask yourself if you can afford to buy that pair of shoes—but it's also awful, really awful, particularly when you feel there is something morally reprehensible about being rich,"[27] as his wife put it—is present too. The sinfully sumptuous banquets of the rich are described at length and at one such feast the good banker, Hugh, "took a sip of Château Magraux, his favorite red wine. It was a lavish wedding breakfast for a special couple, and Hugh was glad he could afford it. But he also felt a twinge of guilt" (*DF* 487), an attitude which parallels Follett's own description of his clothes-buying as "a vice."

It is ultimately in the novels' various and frequent references to Protestantism—to sin, punishment, hard work, Methodism, and retribution—that Follett, I believe, begins to reconcile the apparently contradictory impulses of materialism and asceticism, of Marxism and Christian-Humanism, and ends up appealing to both conservative and liberal readers.

These frequent references start to move *A Dangerous Fortune* in the direction of parable so that the "danger" in the "fortune" is increasingly the worry that a rich man has that he can no more fit through the narrow gates of heaven than a camel can pass through the eye of a needle. As such, it comes as a great relief to Hugh when a financial crash sweeps away his wicked source of wealth and he can live on in joyous poverty: "He smiled: 'We in the lower middle class can't afford to drink spirits. Cocoa is fine'" (559). So too, in *A Place Called Freedom,* the title seems more and more to refer not so much to America but to some paradise beyond the Allegheny Mountains—a Garden of Eden which Mack and Lizzie—or Adam and Eve—attempt to regain.[28]

In the final analysis, both books waver from scene to scene between the contemporary view that "wealth is the power to do good" and the earlier view that "virtue is its own reward," but conclude with a strict Puritan *and* Marxist outlook that money is the root of all evil. Despite Follett's own mixed feelings on this matter, such a conclusion is perhaps inevitable given the indebtedness of melodrama—and the English novel—to *The Pilgrim's Progress,* to medieval morality plays, and to moral exempla.

Part of Follett's success has always resided in his ability to extend the boundaries of a particular genre by drawing from other popular categories and thereby increase his readership. In reviewing *A Dangerous Fortune,* Robert Crampton termed the book a "thriller-saga-historical romance crossover" which is chancy "for a well-recognized writer of male-oriented airport fiction."[29] But such calculated risks lie at the heart of Follett's ability to win new readers. By combining the political novel with the Christian allegory, he deftly appeals to both the Left and the Right, showing us a place where the righteous are progressive and liberal, and where evil is vanquished by the good.

Fittingly, one other novelist who also struggled with melodrama and serious forms, with a Christian mythos and a modern skepticism, and with characters of great evil and great purity, is also one of Follett's models—Thomas Hardy. "What I like to read mostly, for pleasure, are Victorian novels—slow moving, verbose, ponderous, careful novels by Thomas Hardy and Jane Austen." Some of Follett's early and middle novels appeared to have more craft than conviction and he stated at one time: "I bet Hardy wouldn't like my books!"[30] But perhaps Hardy would take a more favorable view of these two recent books because the inclusion of a set of political and ideological values has given to those characters in them a moral complexity and ambiguity that makes them seem human and that adequately addresses Irving Howe's two stated criteria for evaluating a political novel: it must illuminate a portion of our lives and it must provide an ample moral vision (24).

11

CONTINUITY AND CHANGE:
CONCLUSION

By the 1990s, Follett's transformation as a writer was complete, or at least that part of it which had allowed him to move from journalism on an obscure South Wales newspaper to prominence within the British Labour Party. The late-1990s also marked his return to the genre with which he is most associated—the suspense thriller—suggesting that Follett did not so much change the historical novel with his foray into the past as he was changed by it.

As we shall see, Follett's advancement in craft was speeded by his work in historical fiction, which not only allowed for a fuller expression of point-of-view in the sense of attitude or opinion, but also resulted in a fuller control over technique. In fact, a discussion of Follett's use of point-of-view in both meanings of the term, and especially as it has been applied to his two most recent thrillers, becomes essential to understanding his artistic growth as well as the changes he has made to the suspense genre.

In the first place, by gradually shifting the focal point across several of his novels, Follett has shown that the hero of the thriller could be a woman and not, as had largely been the convention, a man. This primary change has raised possibilities for renewal within the genre and is traceable across his various works.

Follett began his career with a sub-Mickey Spillane imitation which relied on the imperative first person point-of-view. Although Follett was already blending-in elements of a counterculture outlook, the novel lapsed frequently into a number of hard-boiled clichés including "tough-guy" banter and images of women as playthings.

His two Piers Roper novels showed a significant advancement of technique. Not only had Follett abandoned the imperative first person point-of-view for the more sophisticated third person limited, but he was attempting to depict a vulnerable, sensitive spy who is changed through contact with women. Although the stories are restricted to Piers' grasp of things, the ideas women share with him play an important part in his moral growth.

With *Eye of the Needle,* Follett moved to an omniscient, or all-knowing, point-of-view, which allowed him to contrast the outlook of strong women characters such as Lucy Rose with obsessive male characters such as Henry Faber. This technique would be continued through his next two novels, *Triple* and *The Key to Rebecca.* Although the women characters play key roles and are capable of heroics when called upon, the battle in these stories is largely between men. The women assist in the resolution of the plot.

This pattern and use of point-of-view begins to change again with *The Man from St. Petersburg* and *Lie Down with Lions.* While the writer still maintains a hovering narrative perspective, moving from male to female to male, much greater emphasis is placed on the social and political consciousness of the women characters, who become speakers for the writer's ideas. Charlotte is saved by her father in *The Man from St. Petersburg,* but Jane Lambert escapes the villain largely on her own; in a sense, she is assisted by Ellis Thaler's plan.

The Pillars of the Earth involves an intricate interplay of good and evil male and female characters, a careful positioning and balancing of parts held together by the all-knowing narrator's point-of-view, by the voice of the historian, the folklorist, and the teller of traditional tales and legends. Although flawed women characters who help the villains had appeared in *The Key to Rebecca* and *The Man from St. Petersburg,* the historical perspective and the resultant distancing from contemporary liberal preconceptions about women allowed Ken Follett in *The Pillars of the Earth* to create a loathsome female character who not only aids the villain but is herself villainous, a technique continued in *A Dangerous Fortune.* While the male characters remain important to the outcome of that story, as does the political perspective of Maisie Robinson, Ken Follett drew a complex, absorbing and memorable portrait of Aunt Augusta, a fierce, manipulative woman who, in the words of one reviewer, "completely takes over [the] novel."[1]

In *The Third Twin* (1996), the change in emphasis from male to female perspective is completed: Jeannie Ferrami is now the true hero of the story, the active, resilient pursuer of the truth and Steve Logan is essentially the secondary character, the one who assists but who is capable of heroics when necessary (a pattern which Follett repeats with Judy Maddox and Michael Quercus in *The Hammer of Eden* [1998]).

While there is much that is familiar in these two recent novels, there is sufficient variation on the form to again suggest growth and renewal. In terms of the many familiar patterns Follett reuses in these two works, a few are worth noting and commenting on briefly since they demonstrate Follett's continued allegiance to a popular literary category as well as his own progression from book to book. These are the presence of social realist concerns (especially in restaurant scenes,[2] though now the woman is largely in control), the use of allegorical elements and symbols, and the specific references to the suspense genre as it had been developed prior to Follett's adoption of the form.

From his early novels, especially *The Big Needle* and the Piers Roper books, Follett transplants an anti-establishment sensibility and an ambivalence toward American materialism—two features of British 1950s' social realism. In *The Third Twin,* Jeannie Ferrami "knew she was not good at dealing with authority figures" (32). In Follett's 1998 novel about counterculture terrorists, *The Hammer of Eden,* the Vietnamese-American FBI agent, Judy Maddox, has contempt for the "suits" and "the big shot[s] from Washington" who are her supervisors (362, 335). The post-war British ambivalence toward American materialism, which Follett had raised in his early works, is present in *The Third Twin* and emphasized in *The Hammer of Eden.* In the more recent book, not only is the perpetrator of the crimes, Ricky "Priest" Granger, an aging leader of a hippie commune who views America as "a wasteland" (22) with "disgusting fast food" (24) but the very plot to destroy a bucolic Northern California town turns the series of actions into something largely symbolic.

As we have noted, one of the strengths of Follett's writing has been his willingness to blend popular and serious forms. In both *The Third Twin* and *The Hammer of Eden,* Follett allows a central metaphor to emerge: just as the island in *Eye of the Needle* had come to represent the isolation of individuals during wartime, the initial sexual violation in *The Third Twin* takes on additional resonances, suggesting a more widespread establishment abuse of women; and the earthquake in *The Hammer of Eden* assumes multiple associations, standing ultimately for the rapid societal changes that the aging hippie leader, Ricky Granger, cannot quite accept (189).

In a clear recycling of the archetypal and allegorical motifs which had appeared in his mid-career novels, the central female character in each of these two more recent books is initially attracted to a false father-figure but grows closer to her biological father as a result of the quest; subsequently, through an encounter with a replacement for the father-figure, she also reawakens to the possibilities of sex and love. Other fairy tale devices used in Follett's mid-career novels are reworked as well: In *The Third Twin,* Jeannie Ferrami crushes the villain's fingers between her teeth (415) and Judy Maddox, in *The Hammer of Eden,* is confronted by a primal scene, resulting in a relative loss of innocence (287). *The Hammer of Eden* even makes specific references to fairy tales (91, 170) in a direct acknowledgement of influences on the text.

In these two books, Follett also acknowledges his popular literary inheritance in a number of key scenes. In addition to the formulaic hunter/hunted device in both novels, Follett includes Buchanesque and Hitchcockian elements. In *The Hammer of Eden,* "all points converge" during a climactic moment (though this is now up-dated to involve helicopters, squad cars and oil-drilling trucks instead of the motor-launches, sail boats and Naval destroyers of *The Thirty-Nine Steps*), and the chase into a public symbol (355) is clearly reminiscent of many such scenes in Alfred Hitchcock films. In *The Third Twin,* Hitchcock's much relied-on storyline of the innocent man falsely accused who must clear himself becomes salient, as does the us/them mentality common to Buchan, Dornford Yates and other espionage writers of the teens and twenties.

Moreover, in the same way that fictional spies from the teens and twenties needed to retain their amateur status through affiliation with a private club, or Peter Cheyney's and Len Deighton's heroes in later decades preserve their integrity through skepticism toward government institutions, Follett's nineties' conspiracy-busters also remain outsiders to the distrusted white male establishment by being female, by quitting or being fired from their jobs, and by their suspicion of the organization itself.

In fact, on several occasions Follett refers directly to his popular cultural inheritance, mentioning the film version of *King Solomon's Mines* in *The Hammer of Eden* (381) and "that Alfred Hitchcock show" in *The Third Twin* (127). References to more contemporary influences occur as well: the evil twin reads Stephen King's *The Dead Zone* in one novel (*TT* 5) while a communard watches *The X-Files* in the other (*HE* 169). When asked about popular influences, Follett has stated that "Ian Fleming has obviously been a big influence on my writing,"[3] and the inclusion of sophisticated technical gadgetry in *The Hammer of Eden* as well as the dastardly scientific plot and a main character's frequently being in danger, captured, and needing to escape in *The Third Twin,* reflect this indebtedness.

But these two books are by no means all repetition and refrain, as a continued discussion of Follett's current use of point-of-view will demonstrate.

In *The Third Twin* in particular, Follett displays a complete technical mastery over vantage point, thus showing his on-going growth as a writer of fiction. The artistic challenge in *The Third Twin,* as the title itself suggests, is to tell the story not just of a central character but of the various good angels and bad angels—the twins—that she will encounter. To create suspense, Follett begins the novel with a blend of third person subjective point-of-view, forcing the reader to participate vicariously in a character's emotions and thoughts, and a third person *objective* stance, which maintains a reserved distance and withholds key information from the reader: "His desire was still strong, but the fantasy was no longer enough. . . . The stranger turned and looked at a display of silver cups in a glass case, trophies won by the Jones Falls athletes" (4/5).

In the next chapter, Follett shifts to a new character, Jeannie Ferrami, and employs an unqualified third person subjective point-of-view to develop complete identification with the character and to establish her reliability. Told without irony, her perceptions are presumably our perceptions; she will become our anchor and *raisonneure* in the narrative:

Jeannie took longer, washing her hair. She was grateful for Lisa's friendship. . . . Jeannie liked working with Lisa in the lab because she was completely reliable; and she liked hanging out with her after work because she felt she could say whatever came into her mind without fear of shocking her. (20/21)

There is no implied distance between author and character in this section, and the reader must assume that Lisa is indeed reliable and unflappable because the central character, Jeannie, has so concluded.

This is not the case in the third chapter, which gives us yet another point-of-view: that of the vain, bombastic senior professor, Berrington Jones:

He studied his image and liked what he saw. He was in reality a short man, but television made everyone the same height. His navy suit looked good, the sky blue shirt matched his eyes, and the tie was a burgundy red that did not flare on the screen. Being supercritical, he thought his silver hair was too neat, almost bouffant: he was in danger of looking like a television evangelist. (37)

Here again, Follett uses a blend of authorial objectivity—"He was in reality short man" who was "supercritical"—and the subjective perceptions of the character himself: "[H]e liked what he saw" but "thought his silver hair was too neat." In this case, the combination of inner and outer narration is not being used to create mystery or to withhold important information (such as the identity of the rapist in the first chapter) but to negate the dependability of the character's perceptions. His conclusions are not ours because we have been told otherwise; the author even implies that Jones probably does look like a television preacher since much of the paragraph establishes his denial of realities.

These deft touches show Follett's present skill in establishing varied points-of-view, and while he had attempted something similar in the early caper *Paper Money,* in that novel the narrative voice throughout the text and across characters remained essentially the same. In *The*

Third Twin, on the other hand, Follett positions a new character and a distinctive character perspective at the beginning of each of the first four chapters (Steve Logan is developed as a reliable consciousness in the fourth chapter) and can then proceed to alternate these various perspectives throughout the text. The artistic dilemma, of course, will result from the demands of suspense-fiction writing where at some juncture all plots—or in this case, all points-of-view—must intersect. So long as each character can express a perspective and attitude in separate chapters, there is no confusion or disorientation for the reader, but in *The Third Twin* Follett presents himself with the challenge of placing the perspectives of "two completely different individuals—one a charming college boy, the other a psychopath" (146) next to Jeannie's.

Here, Follett will resort not so much to the devices of suspense-fiction writing, but to the methods of Modernism to resolve this issue.

We have seen that Follett, in his early writing, alternately toyed with the techniques of Modernism and deliberately rejected them. In early works, when such techniques as stream-of-consciousness or interior monologue were included, these often seemed arbitrarily applied and somewhat inconsistent: this was certainly the case in *The Bear Raid* and *The Key to Rebecca* where the techniques were not really demanded by the necessities of plot. Although dream imagery and the occasional Modernist interlude occur in *Eye of the Needle* and *Triple,* the tendency in Follett's writing was *away* from introspection and psychological associations, as his 1979 essay on "Books That Enchant and Entertain" made clear.

Now, however, it is the interior monologue which allows Follett to intensify suspense in several key scenes toward the end of the novel. In an encounter between Jeannie and the evil twin, the reader is allowed, through the device of the conversation with the self, to know what the evil twin is thinking while Jeannie is kept outside his thought process, thus making her seem particularly vulnerable: "He had no idea what she was talking about. *Oh, Christ, I've made a slip.* He looked around the apartment: no stereo. *Dumb*" (408). Later, Steve Logan will penetrate Professor Jones' sanctum and Follett will use a similar device to dramatize the game of wits: "Steve was about to say 'Yes' when he caught the trace of a puzzled frown on Berrington's face. *Is this a test? Is Barack suspicious?*" (431).

Follett, in the interests of consistency and the even application of technique, will also include Jeannie's interior monologue (294) and Berrington Jones' (449) so that the reader has a clear understanding of what each of the key characters would like to know: namely, what the other characters are thinking. Since this device is introduced well in advance of the climactic scenes, the reader is not only prepared for such authorial shifts but willing to accept them as a convention of the novel.

In addition, the use of interior monologue (rather than omniscience, which had been the device for the central encounters in *The Key to Rebecca* and *Triple*) is dramatically as well as thematically motivated in *The Third Twin:* "Steve tried to see beyond Harvey's appearance, read his face and look into his heart, and see the cancer that made him evil. But he could not" (460). Evil, as in Iago's case, remains mute and enigmatic and can only be guessed at. The use of interior monologue, however, has allowed the reader a fuller understanding of character, which is the essence of drama.

Point-of-view is used somewhat differently in *The Hammer of Eden* and for slightly different artistic purposes. The novel begins with an italicized dream sequence, written in the present tense and with some of the devices of third person interior monologue—strong sense impressions, reflection and doubt, discovery of one's self or one's surroundings—and ends with a similar italicized sequence, though this is now told as the present tense reality. Within the body of the text, however, the novel relies on anonymous narration to alternate the perspectives of Judy Maddox, the terrorist-catcher, and Ricky "Priest" Granger, the leader of a fringe group determined to prevent the building of a hydro-electric dam. As with *Eye of the Needle,* which carefully moved from the spy's story to the spycatcher's in ever shorter segments, The *Hammer of Eden* as well first allocates entire chapters to Judy's or Ricky's contrasting perspectives, then combines the dual viewpoint within a single chapter to quicken the pace (286), and finally, in the climactic scene, cuts back and forth from paragraph to paragraph (392).

In fact, this use of alternating perspectives is actually much more skillfully managed than it had been in *Eye of the Needle* and in other mid-career thrillers where Follett would include the observations of Hitler or of Anwar Sadat to bring in the international consequences. Although the use of multiple perspectives had allowed Follett in those earlier works to draw from different kinds of novels to create a single blend, by limiting the point-of-view to only two key characters in *The Hammer of Eden* Follett can create sharper contrasts and can, in fact, direct the reader more deliberately toward authorial attitude. As Janet Burroway has noted, an "author inevitably wants to convince us to share the same [view of the world]" and this "will ultimately be revealed by his or her manipulation of the technique of point-of-view."[4]

In Follett's case, the strict use of a dual perspective allows for the re-narration of key scenes so that readers can be more specifically guided in their sympathies. When a Northern California town, described as a cluster of fast-food restaurants, chapels and office buildings (*HE* 320), is destroyed by Ricky Granger, the reader is first asked to share vicariously in his triumph and to gloat in the symbolic destruction of American small-town smugness (322). But when the same scene is re-told from Judy Maddox's perspective, "her view changed" (322), as does the reader's. Within the space of a page, words such as "shocking," "horror," "gasped" and "dreadful" (322-33) occur to remind the reader of how one should appropriately feel.

Second, the narrative perspective allows for the steady layering of character in ways that recall the best parts of *Eye of the Needle*. Roderick MacLeish's praise for Follett's 1978 bestseller could as easily be applied to his 1998 book, since in both cases Follett brings the villain "slowly to life, developing and complicating him with a skillful leisure."[5] Follett's sympathy for the causes of the Left are well known and this perhaps results in an identification with the radical environmentalist, Ricky Granger, that was not entirely possible toward the Nazi spy, Henry Faber. Ricky's attitudes are expressed from his own perspective and without the distancing technique of authorial irony: "[He] believed the public were their own censors. They refused to buy newspapers or watch TV shows that challenged their prejudices, so they got fed pap" (*HE* 177). Other members of the commune profess a late-1960s ideology, again without authorial interruption, so that the statement "we believed that our parents had made a society that was twisted and corrupt and poi-soned" (24) is left unchallenged. Even the violent activities of this fringe group are, to a certain extent, presented as justifiable, especially since their point-of-view, in both senses of the term, dominates specific sec-tions:

"We're not criminals," Star said forcefully. "We're trying to save the coun-try."

"Damn right," Priest said with a smile, and he punched the air.

"I mean it," she said. "In a hundred years' time, when the people look back, they'll say we're the rational ones, and the government was insane for let-ting America be destroyed by pollution. Like deserters in World War One—they were hated then, but nowadays everybody says the men who ran away were the only ones who weren't mad."

Oaktree said: "That's the truth." (314)

Follett forces an identification with Ricky Granger in other ways as well. In addition to using italicized interior monologue to put us inside a character's consciousness, a technique he had effectively employed in *The Third Twin*, Follett now uses that device to express Granger's doubts and second thoughts. As a result, he becomes, like Henry Faber in *Eye of the Needle,* a reluctant killer in desperate circumstances, one who (we are told in authorial narration) "was willing to do anything to save the commune, but he knew it would be smarter to avoid killing if he could" (*HE* 283). We have seen that Follett could not sustain the trick of making the villain the hero in *Eye of the Needle*. Perhaps here he has, to the slight detriment of the book.

James Moffett and Kenneth McElheny have noted in their discussion of "Anonymous Narration—Dual Character Point of View" that "one character's point of view may clearly dominate the other's, in extent or importance,"[6] and this is what noticeably happens in *The Hammer of Eden*. Not only are Priest's chapters longer and more complex than are Judy Maddox's (chapter 9, for example, which gives us Priest's outlook, is 25 pages long, compared to the ten and a half pages that comprise Judy's perspective in chapter 10), but Priest's ancestry is considerably more complicated and more effectively explored through the third person limited technique.

Although Judy Maddox is described as Vietnamese-American, little is made of her ethnicity except her ability to wear tight-fitting traditional garments that show off "her shoulder-length black hair and honey-colored skin" and that flatter "her petite figure" (63). Several scenes take place in restaurants: Judy walks into "the sophisticated ambience of Masa's, wearing a black silk sheath and row of pearls" (92), which suggests that in Follett's recent novels set in the United States, American life continues to be viewed through the prism of social class. In consequence, Follett essentially misses the opportunity to explore the characterization of Judy and the way she might genuinely see herself as divided. Instead, her world view has more to do with career advancement, the need to make more money, and her observation that her father's house was in a neighborhood that "was not very swanky, but [then] an honest cop never got rich" (63).

On the other hand, Priest's self-image and attitudes toward wealth are more directly the result of his biography. Follett has indicated that a character in a novel who is deeply committed to a cause must have inherited that idealism either directly or indirectly.[7] Just as Henry Faber's devotion to his country was the result of his being high-born, well-educated, and a star student, Ricky "Priest" Granger's hatred for the suburban middle class is in part the outcome of his being a school dropout, illiterate, and uncertain of who his real father was.

Granger, in fact, maintains the fantasy that his biological father was a traveling Englishman who would come back one day "in a big limousine loaded with presents" (381). In addition to this oblique reference to disparities of wealth in Britain, the connection between Granger and certain British antecedents is even stronger when one considers his literary ancestors in Follett's popular novels. Granger shares much with the professional criminal Tony Cox in *Paper Money,* who learned to steal food "scraps from under [market] tables to sell to the soap factory for a few coppers" (60), and with the jewel thief Harry Marks in *Night Over Water,* who had grown up "in a tenement in Battersea . . . , had a knack of escaping from trouble" (47) and who later ends up on the run in North America. Granger, as well, "had never lived straight, had been brought up in a whorehouse, educated on the streets [and was] briefly the owner of a semilegitimate business" (*HE* 142). In the context of Follett's work overall, Granger starts to appear as a sort of exiled Englishman in the American wilderness,[8] anachronistically using an old Western six-shooter, but a character whose world view and whose railing against suburban America is more authentically linked to background and to social class.

Moreover, through the careful use of the historian's point-of-view, Follett continues to deepen the characterization of Granger as part of a dying breed. While Follett had used the voice of the historian in *Eye of the Needle* and in *The Key to Rebecca,* he had almost certainly improved its use through the writing of true historical novels—*The Pillars of the Earth, A Dangerous Fortune,* and *A Place Called Freedom.* Now, instead of constructing the historical perspective as a separable section, which he had done in *Eye,* Follett combines it with Ricky Granger's interior monologue or diction to give the reader an added perspective and a sense of the 1960s' counterculture movement as an episode and as a part of history. We are told, for example, that "[a]t the peak of the hippie era, [Star] had lived in the Haight-Ashbury neighborhood of San Francisco. Priest had not known her then—he had spent the late sixties making his first million dollars—but he had heard the stories" (11). The chronicler's style allows a reader to see historical events as if they were taking place presently, while being reminded through the past perfect tense that they are long over. In a sense, through the historical viewpoint, Granger is depicted as someone who also re-sees his life presently but who dimly recognizes too that those formative years are since past.

This closeness to Ricky Granger results, finally, in an extra demand on the plot. Follett has remarked that the "bad guys are always more fun to write than the good guys,"[9] but the sympathy—perhaps even strong identification—with an aging counterculture figure makes the writer seemingly reluctant to end the novel according to the necessities of plot. Instead, there are two endings—one required by the genre and the other the consequence of authorial outlook—and two epilogues; the first making use of the historian's comfortable perspective to suggest that all is right in the world, and the second relying on the more unsettling Modernist monologue in the present tense. This intricate use of point-of-view again expresses the author's outlook by implying that the spirit of the 1960s, if not the methods of extremist groups, remains viable and immediate.

As we have seen in this study, Follett's recent advancement in craft is to a large extent the result of his work in historical fiction, which allowed both for a fuller expression of political ideology as well as an accelerated shift of focal point toward a central female character. We have also noted Follett's admiration for 19th-century novelists such as Jane Austen and Thomas Hardy, who also created believable, enduring, and complex female characters. This connection leads us to a second major change that Follett has effected: By dipping into the eras that Austen and Hardy had described, Follett returned from his own Georgian and Victorian historical novels better able to point to a new direction in the thriller form—the woman's thriller—a direction that might have been the spy story's from the very beginning had it been based on the reality of espionage rather than on the schoolboy adventure fantasies that had formed the core of Buchan's and Childer's youthful reading.

James Fenimore Cooper created the fictional character, Harvey Birch, who was a double agent during the Revolutionary War, but the most successful actual spy during the War of Independence was the American woman, Patience Wright, who infiltrated the Royal Court. Between the years that Wilkie Collins advanced the development of mystery and detective fiction with *The Woman in White* in 1860 and *The Moonstone* in 1868, two actual women agents pursued real secrets for their respective sides during the American Civil War—Elizabeth van Lew as an agent for the North and Belle Boyd, who worked for the South. At the time that John Buchan was writing his hearty adventure in which the fictional Richard Hannay outwits a gang of German spies and is rewarded for his exploits with a captain's commission, Gertrude Margaret Zelle ("Mata Hari") was found guilty of espionage and was executed by a French firing squad. Second World War and post-war espionage fiction often put the "thrill" in the thriller by placing fictional secret agents such as Alec Leamas and Harry Palmer behind enemy lines, but historical Odette Sansom, Violet Szabo, and "Christine Granville" all worked behind the lines for British Intelligence and received awards for bravery.[10]

Espionage and thriller writers even as late as John Le Carré and Charles McCarry have tended to ignore this reality in favor of the equally great or perhaps even more numerous incidents of male heroism behind enemy lines; as we have seen, another reality had been that up until the 1970s most readers of espionage fiction were men.

Follett has changed all that. By carefully drawing female readers to the form through market-place targeting and through the inclusion of strong female characters, he has considerably extended the genre. As such, he not only represents a post-Ian Fleming sensibility toward the thriller form, but a post-John Le Carré approach as well. In 1991, Follett stated that Le Carré, as a novelist, "is getting old" and while this harsh remark was in response to an equally acerbic comment that Follett is a "mediocre writer,"[11] it does suggest a generational conflict and implies that Follett might view John Le Carré's saga of aging bureaucrats in an aging institution as fundamentally passé.

To a generation of thriller writers born since the war, Follett has pointed to the possibilities for renewal within the form. Daniel Silva's 1996 bestseller *An Unlikely Spy* seemed so patterned on Follett's *Eye of the Needle* as to raise accusations of plagiarism.[12] Both novels are about a German spy in wartime London who discovers the secret of the Normandy invasion. Both stories have history professors who are recruited into Military Intelligence as spycatchers; both spycatchers are after upper-class Prussian agents who kill their victims with stiletto knives and then become sick. But Daniel Silva, as if parodying Follett's writing in the 1990s instead of the 1970s, has made an incremental adjustment to the plot: his Henry Faber is now a woman.

Follett has made one other major contribution to the thriller form: he has pointed out to younger writers the possibility for the inclusion of the theme of love in suspense fiction.

That this contribution to popular literature should come from a male writer who had long been restricted, in Britain at least, to the action-adventure men's market is perhaps ironic, given the extensive list of women writers of category fiction. Mystery and detective fiction, for example, which flowered before and developed quite separately from espionage fiction, has included many notable women practitioners, from Baroness Orczy through Agatha Christie and Dorothy Sayers to Josephine Tey and P. D. James; but these writers generally omitted love stories from their mysteries, either treating romantic couples comically (as was the case with Agatha Christie and Georgette Heyer during the "Golden Age" of mysteries) or focusing on the consequences of flawed domestic arrangements, as is the approach of contemporary women mystery writers such as P. D. James and Ruth Rendell.

Perhaps because few women writers have worked in the espionage category, this change would be left to a man whose political and social conscience was formed in the 1960s and who has frequently emphasized his identification with women "able enough to overcome the sexism of [their] era."[13] Margery Allingham, a writer from the "Golden Age" whose anti-Nazi mystery *Traitor's Purse* (1941) contains both espionage and romance elements, only fully engaged the theme of love toward the end of her career and in non-thriller or detective stories. Even Helen MacInnes, probably the most notable woman espionage writer, tended not to highlight romance in her novels. In *Assignment in Brittany* (1942), a love affair is a plot complication rather than its resolution; her 1960 novel *Decision at Delphi* ends with a reassuring embrace, but the novel had not been about love.

It was left to Ken Follett to resolve a fundamental dilemma facing espionage writers, men and women both. As Josh Rubins noted in his review of a Follett novel, "the more substantial, ambitious sort of international suspense, which depends on a certain tough-minded realism, often stumbles into mawkishness and damsel-in-distress twitterings when it gives central importance to romance." Rubins found Follett's first major thriller to be "an impressively canny exception" and observed that Follett had included the pattern of romance in his subsequent thrillers.[14]

In consequence, the love story element today is not so much the exception as the rule. Not only does Daniel Silva's novel employ a love relationship as part of the plot, but as formulaic a writer as Jeffrey Archer now ends his two spy thrillers, *A Matter of Honor* (1986) and *Honor Among Thieves* (1993), with an implied marriage, believing, perhaps, that in the genre as amended by Ken Follett, romance is not so much antithetical to the purposes of the spy writer, but a central ingredient.

NOTES

Preface

1. Harvey Pekar, "Getting Serious About the Funnies," *Chicago Tribune,* 21 Jan. 1996, sec. 14: 9.

2. Bruce Merry, *Anatomy of the Spy Thriller* (Montreal: McGill, 1977), 50. Other useful histories of the British spy thriller include LeRoy Panek's *The Special Branch: The British Spy Novel, 1890-1980* (Bowling Green, OH: Bowling Green State University Popular Press, 1981), and John G. Cawelti and Bruce Rosenberg's *The Spy Story* (Chicago: University of Chicago Press, 1987).

3. H. J. Kirchhoff, "Thriller Writer Turns His Hand to Historical Romance," review of *The Pillars of the Earth, Toronto Globe and Mail,* 12 Sept. 1989, sec. 1: 25.

4. Roderick MacLeish, "Finely Stitched Thriller," *Book World: The Washington Post,* 2 July 1978: 4.

5. Carol Lawson, "Behind the Bestsellers," *New York Times,* 15 July 1978, sec. 7: 24; Paul Hendrickson, "Ken Follett's Winging Ways," *Washington Post Book World,* 21 Sept. 1983, sec. 3: 1.

6. MacLeish, "Finely Stitched," 1; Paul Nathan, "Dell Pays 12.3 Million for Two Follett Books," *Publishers' Weekly,* 13 July 1990: 9; Cawelti and Rosenberg, *Spy Story,* 242.

7. Kirchhoff, "Thriller Writer," 25.

8. Andrew F. and Gina Macdonald, *Dictionary of Literary Biography,* 1987 ed., s.v. "Follett, Ken."

9. Richard C. Turner, *Ken Follett: A Critical Companion* (Westport, CT: Greenwood, 1996), 27.

Chapter 1: Introduction and Overview

1. Martin Jacques, "Ken and Barbie," *Sunday Times Magazine* (London), 19 Sept. 1993: 50-53.

2. Marian Christy, "Ken Follett: Master of Suspense," *Boston Globe,* 16 Oct. 1991, Living Section: 39; *Current Biography,* 1990 ed., s.v. "Follett, Ken"; Jacques, "Ken and Barbie," 51; "Influences," *New Statesman and Society,* 1 July 1994: 13.

3. Richard Rodriguez, *Hunger of Memory* (1982; reprint, New York: Bantam, 1983), 46-73.

4. Broadcast, PBS, 6 July 1980; Interviews by Bryant Gumbel, *Today Show,* NBC-TV, 4 Feb. 1986 and 24 Sept. 1991.

5. Rodriguez, *Hunger,* 67.

6. See the following, in particular: Henri C. Veit, "Fiction," review of *Triple, Library Journal,* 1 Nov. 1979: 2376; Peter Andrews, "Three Stooges in Cairo . . . ," review of *The Key to Rebecca, New York Times Book Review,* 21 Sept. 1989: 9; Jane Spitzer, review of *Lie Down with Lions, Christian Science Monitor,* 11 Feb. 1986: 24; Frederick Busch, "Follett's Spy Story Pays Off Only for Author," review of *The Key to Rebecca, Chicago Tribune,* 5 Oct. 1980, sec. 7: 6.

7. Macdonald, "Follett," 114.

8. Ken Follett, "Books That Enchant and Entertain," *The Writer,* June 1979: 9; Christy, "Master," 39.

9. Leo Lowenthal, *Literature, Popular Culture, and Society* (Englewood Cliffs, NJ: Prentice Hall, 1961), 131; Christy, "Master," 39.

10. *Authors and Artists for Young People,* 1991 ed., s.v. "Follett, Ken"; Rider McDowell, "Focus on: Ken Follett," *Espionage,* Oct. 1986: 96; Christy, "Master," 39.

11. Ken Follett [Symon Myles, pseud.], *The Big Needle* (London: Everest Books, 1974; reprinted under the name Ken Follett, New York: Zebra, 1979), 107. All subsequent quotations or page citations from *The Big Needle* refer to the reprint edition.

12. Christy, "Master," 39.

13. McDowell, "Focus," 96.

14. Follett, "Enchant," 11; Ken Follett [Bernard L. Ross, pseud.], *Capricorn One* (London: Futura, 1978), 7. All subsequent quotations or page citations from *Capricorn One* refer to this edition.

15. Ken Follett, introduction to *Paper Money* (New York: NAL Signet, 1987), vi; H. R. F. Keating, "Crime," review of *The Modigliani Scandal,* by Ken Follett [Zachary Stone, pseud.], *Times* (London), 22 Jan. 1976: 17.

16. Ken Follett [Zachary Stone, pseud.], *The Modigliani Scandal* (London: Collins, 1976; reprinted under the name Ken Follett, New York: NAL Signet, 1985), 138. All subsequent quotations or page citations from *The Modigliani Scandal* refer to the reprint edition.

17. Gary Dretzka, " 'Paper Money' Provides Good Value," review of *Paper Money, Chicago Tribune,* 25 Oct. 1987, sec. 6: 14.

18. Ken Follett [Zachary Stone, pseud.], *Paper Money* (London: Collins, 1977; reprinted under the name Ken Follett, New York: NAL Signet, 1987), 63. All subsequent quotations or page citations from *Paper Money* refer to the reprint edition.

19. Follett, intro, *Paper,* vi.

20. Ken Follett, *Eye of the Needle* (published in England as *Storm Island:* Macdonald and Janes, 1978; reprint, New York: Arbor House, 1978), 22. All subsequent quotations or page citations from *Eye of the Needle* refer to this

reprint (hardbound) edition.

21. Peter Prescott, "Stop That Man!" review of *Eye of the Needle, Newsweek,* 7 Aug. 1978: 76.

22. Josh Rubin, "Between C.I.A. and K.G.B. in Afghanistan," review of *Lie Down with Lions, New York Times Book Review,* 26 Jan. 1986, sec. 7: 9; *Authors and Artists,* 1991 ed.; Connie Lauerman, "Novelist Follett Tests His Wings," review of *On Wings of Eagles, Chicago Tribune,* 19 Oct. 1983, sec. 5: 1; Ken Follett, *On Wings of Eagles* (New York: Morrow, 1983), 9. All subsequent quotations or page citations from *On Wings of Eagles* refer to this edition; Lauerman, "Novelist," 1; Don Campbell, "Tehran Rescue: A Real-Life Thriller," review of *On Wings of Eagles, Los Angeles Times,* 11 Sept. 1983: 16.

23. Ken Follett, *Lie Down with Lions* (London: Hamilton, 1985; reprint, New York: NAL Signet, 1986), 6. All subsequent quotations or page citations from *Lie Down with Lions* refer to the reprint edition.

24. Jacques, "Ken and Barbie," 52; Ken Follett, "On the Altar of Overlord," review of *Fall from Grace,* by Larry Collins, *New York Times,* 16 June 1985: 14; Turner, *Companion,* 7.

25. Follett, "Altar," 14; Kirchhoff, "Thriller Writer," 25.

26. Ken Follett, *The Pillars of the Earth* (New York: Morrow, 1989; reprint, New York: NAL Signet, 1989), 19. All subsequent quotations or page citations from *The Pillars of the Earth* refer to the reprint edition.

27. Jean H. Ross, "Ken Follett: CA Interview," *Contemporary Authors,* New Revision Series, 1985, 33:153; Kirchhoff, "Thriller Writer," 25.

28. Gumbel, Interview, 24 Sept. 1991; Ken Follett, *Night Over Water* (New York: Morrow, 1991), 29. All subsequent quotations or page citations from *Night Over Water* refer to this edition.

29. Ken Follett, *The Third Twin* (New York: Crown, 1996; reprint, New York: Fawcett Crest, 1997), 110. All subsequent quotations or page citations from *The Third Twin* refer to the reprint edition. Where needed for clarity, the abbreviation *TT* is used within parenthetical citations.

30. Ken Follett, *A Dangerous Fortune* (New York: Morrow, 1993; reprint, New York: Dell, 1993), 201. All subsequent quotations or page citations from *A Dangerous Fortune* refer to the reprint edition. Where needed for clarity, the abbreviation *DF* is used within parenthetical citations.

31. Ken Follett, *A Place Called Freedom* (New York: Crown, 1995; reprint, New York: Fawcett Crest, 1995), 162. All subsequent quotations or page citations from *A Place Called Freedom* refer to the reprint edition. Where needed for clarity, the abbreviation *PC* is used within parenthetical citations.

32. Macdonald, "Follett," 114.

33. "Keeping the Plot Turning," *Bookseller,* 8 Sept. 1995: 68.

34. Ken Follett, *The Hammer of Eden* (New York: Crown, 1998), 10. All subsequent quotations or page citations from *The Hammer of Eden* refer to this

edition. Where needed for clarity, the abbreviation *HE* is used within parenthetical citations.

35. John Braine, *Writing a Novel* (New York: Coward, McCann and Geoghegan, 1974), 132; Ken Follett, "Capitalism, Socialism and Radio Wawa," *Bookseller,* 18 Sept. 1992: 826.

H.R.F. Keating, in a review of a very early Follett novel, noted that *The Bear Raid* was a "bit overloaded with events, and sex." T. J. Binyon, writing for the *Times Literary Supplement* in 1980, asked for "more concentration on intelligence work, and less on sexual perversion," a sentiment echoed by Jane Spitzer a few years later when she argued in a *Christian Science Monitor* review that *Lie Down with Lions* was "marred by an explicit and completely gratuitous sex scene." As recently as 1996, a reviewer suggested that "Follett's only mistake [in *The Third Twin*] is an overemphasis on sexual violence, which taints an otherwise excellent book." Keating, "Crime," *Times* (London), 27 May 1976: 10; T. J. Binyon, "Crime," review of *The Key to Rebecca, Times Literary Supplement,* 26 Dec. 1980: 1458; Spitzer, review of *Lions,* 24; Tom Regan, "Books," review of *The Third Twin, Christian Science Monitor,* 14 Nov. 1996: 14.

36. Lauerman, "Novelist," 3.

Chapter 2: Writing as "Symon Myles"

1. Christy, "Master," 39.

2. John F. Baker, "PW Interviews Ken Follett," *Publishers' Weekly,* 17 Jan. 1986: 55.

3. "Influences," 13; Jacques, "Ken and Barbie," 51.

4. Dennis Kavanagh, "Political Culture in Great Britain: The Decline of Civic Culture," *The Civic Culture Revisited,* ed. G. A. Almond and S. Verba (Boston: Little, Brown, 1980), 170.

5. Kenneth Van Dover, *Murder in the Millions* (New York: Ungar, 1984), 5. All subsequent quotations or page citations from *Murder in the Millions* refer to this edition.

6. Hendrickson, "Winging Ways," 1; *Current Biography,* 1990 ed.

7. Robert McCrum, William Cran, and Robert MacNeil, *The Story of English* (New York: Viking, 1986), 33.

8. Follett, "Enchant," 9.

9. Jeff Guin, "In the Beginning Was the Word, and the Word Was Published!" *Fort Worth Star Telegram,* 3 Dec. 1995, Life Section: 1; Barbara Isenberg, "No Cheap Thrillers from Follett's Pen," *Los Angeles Times,* 1 Oct. 1980, sec. 4: 5; McDowell, "Focus," 94;

10. John Cawelti, *Adventure, Mystery, and Romance* (Chicago: University of Chicago Press, 1976), 188-89. All subsequent quotations or page citations from *Adventure, Mystery and Romance* refer to this edition.

11. McDowell, "Focus," 98.

12. Jacques, "Ken and Barbie," 51.

13. Mickey Spillane, *Vengeance Is Mine* (1950; reprint, New York: Penguin, 1978), 51. All other quotations from *Vengeance Is Mine* refer to this edition.

14. Phillip Norton, *The British Polity* (New York: Longman, 1984), 34.

15. Alan Marsh, *Protest and Political Consciousness* (Beverly Hills, CA: Sage, 1977), 118.

16. Anthony Birch, *The British System of Government,* 9th ed. (London: Routledge, 1993), 22.

17. Baker, "PW Interviews," 55; McDowell, "Focus," 96.

18. Graham Greene, *The Pleasure Dome: Collected Film Criticism 1935-40,* ed. John Russell Taylor (1972; reprint, London: Oxford University Press, 1980), 60.

19. Geoffrey Household, *Rogue Male* (1939; reprint, London: Penguin, 1977), 40-42.

20. For a discussion of Buchan's indebtedness to Bunyan's *The Pilgrim's Progress,* see Jeanne F. Bedell, "Romance and Moral Certainty: The Espionage Fiction of John Buchan," *Midwest Quarterly,* 22 (Spring 1981): 230-41.

21. Joseph Conrad, "The Heart of Darkness" (1902; reprint, New York: NAL Signet, 1980), 66; John Le Carré [David Cornwell], *A Perfect Spy* (New York: Knopf, 1986), 124.

Tennyson's "In Memoriam," in particular, where " 'the stars,' she whispers, 'blindly run' " and where "Nature, red in tooth and claw with ravine, shrieked against his creed."

22. Jacques, "Ken and Barbie," 51; *Authors and Artists,* 1991 ed.; McDowell, "Focus," 97.

23. Tom Ryall, *Alfred Hitchcock and British Cinema* (Beckenham, England: Croom Helm, 1986), 119.

24. Follett, "Altar," 14.

Chapter 3: The "Mystery" of Early Success

1. Baker, "PW Interviews," 55. This was particularly the case in the late 1980s, when Follett made the comment. He has indicated since then that he is becoming better known in Britain, though this may to some extent be the result of the public role he has played in the British Labour Party. See chap. 1, n. 33.

2. McDowell, "Focus," 98.

3. Phillip Marchand, "Ken Follett Turns His Magic Hand to Historical Fiction," *Toronto Star,* 29 Sept. 1994, sec. 4: 10; Michael Adams, *Dictionary of Literary Biography Yearbook: 1981,* 1982 ed., s.v. "Follett, Ken."

4. Ken Follett, introduction to *The Shakeout* (London: Harwood Smith, 1975; reprint, New York: Armchair Detective, 1990), i. All subsequent quota-

tions and page references from the introduction or the text of *The Shakeout* refer to the reprint edition. Where needed for clarity, the abbreviation *SK* is used within parenthetical citations.

5. Cawelti and Rosenberg, *Spy Story,* 3.

6. Follett, "Enchant," 10; *Authors and Artists,* 1991 ed.

7. Stuart Laing, *"Room at the Top* and the Morality of Affluence," *Popular Fiction and Social Change,* ed. Christopher Pawling (New York: St. Martin's, 1984), 158.

8. Cawelti and Rosenberg, *Spy Story,* 83.

9. *Current Biography,* 1990 ed.

10. John Buchan, *The 39 Steps* (1915; reprint, New York: Popular Library, 1961), 130; John Le Carré, *Tinker, Tailor, Soldier, Spy* (New York: Knopf, 1974; reprint, Bantam, 1975), 347.

11. Ken Follett, *The Bear Raid* (London: Harwood-Smith, 1976; reprint, New York: Armchair Detective, 1990), 83. All subsequent quotations or page citations from *The Bear Raid* refer to the reprint edition. Where needed for clarity, the abbreviation *BR* is used within parenthetical citations.

12. Richard Usborne, *Clubland Heroes: A Nostalgic Study of Some Recurrent Characters in the Romantic Fiction of Dornford Yates, John Buchan, and "Sapper."* (London: Constable, 1953); David Cannadine, "James Bond and the Decline of England," *Encounter,* 53 (Sept. 1979): 46-55.

13. Le Carré, *Tinker, Tailor,* 347/345.

14. E. Phillips Oppenheim, *The Secret . . .* (London: Ward, Lock and Co., 1907), 52.

15. Additional evidence also suggests that Ken Follett did not make his first trip to the United States until 1978, as part of the publicity for *Eye of the Needle* (see Carol Lawson, "Behind the Bestsellers," *New York Times,* 15 July 1978, sec. 7: 24; Thomas Lask, "Publishing: The Making of a Big Book," *New York Times,* 12 May 1978, sec. 3: 26; McDowell, "Focus," 96.)

16. John Spurling, *Graham Greene* (London: Methuen, 1983), 54.

17. Lauerman, "Novelist," 1.

18. Ken Follett [Martin Martinsen, pseud.], *The Power Twins and the Worm Puzzle* (London: Abelard, 1976; reprinted under the name Ken Follett, New York: Morrow Junior Books, 1990), 46. All subsequent quotations or page citations from *The Power Twins* refer to the reprint edition.

19. David Craig, afterword to *Saturday Night and Sunday Morning,* by Alan Sillitoe (London: Longman, 1976), 229-30.

20. Jacques, "Ken and Barbie," 52.

21. Laing, "Affluence," 158.

22. Craig, afterword to *Saturday Night,* 217; John Braine, *Room at the Top* (1957; reprint, Harmondsworth, England, 1975), 41.

23. Laing, "Affluence," 162.

24. Allan J. Mayer, "High Noon in Egypt," review of *The Key to Rebecca, Newsweek,* 29 Sept. 1980: 83; Macdonald, "Follett," 114.

25. Jane S. Bakerman, *Twentieth-Century Crime and Mystery Writers,* 1991 ed., s.v. "Follett, Ken."

26. Ken Follett, "The Spy as Hero and Villain," *The Murder Mystique: Crime Writers on Their Art,* ed. Lucy Freeman (New York: Frederick Ungar, 1982), 77.

27. Macdonald, "Follett," 120; Marchand, "Magic Hand," 10; Janette Johnson, "Ken Follett," *Contemporary Authors,* New Revision Series, 1985, 33:150; Adams, "Follett," 203.

28. Jacques, "Ken and Barbie," 52.

29. Mordecai Richler, review of *Life at the Top,* by John Braine, *The Spectator,* 19 Oct. 1962: 602.

30. Isenberg, "Thrillers," 1; Robert Crampton, "Putting the Social in Socialism," *Sunday Times Magazine* (London), 9 July 1994: 9; McDowell, "Focus," 94.

31. Hendrickson, "Winging Ways," 3; Baker, "PW Interviews," 55; Crampton, "Social," 11.

32. Isenberg, "Thrillers," 5.

Chapter 4: An Eye for Literature

1. Follett, intro, *Paper Money,* v.

2. Peter M. Gareffa, "Ken Follett," *Contemporary Authors,* New Revision Series, 1985, 33:188; McDowell, "Focus," 94.

3. Baker, "PW Interviews," 55.

4. Gareffa, "Follett," 188.

5. Lauerman, "Novelist," 3.

6. *Current Biography,* 1990 ed.; Macdonald, "Follett," 117; Paul Nathan, "Dell Pays," 9.

7. MacLeish, "Finely Stitched," 1; review of *Eye of the Needle, Time,* 30 Oct. 1978: 135; Richard Freedman, review of *Eye of the Needle, New York Times Book Review,* 16 July 1978: 18; Prescott, "Stop That Man!" 76.

8. Follett, "Enchant," 9-11.

9. H. R. F. Keating, "Crime," review of *Storm Island,* by Ken Follett, *Times* (London), 3 Aug. 1978: 12.

10. Tom Harrison, *Living through the Blitz* (Harmondsworth, England: Penguin, 1978), 15.

11. MacLeish, "Finely Stitched," 4; Keating, rev. *Storm,* 12; Wayne Booth, "Distance and Point of View: An Essay in Classification," *The Theory of the Novel,* ed. Phillip Stevick (New York: Free Press, 1967), 97.

12. Follett, "Enchant," 10.

13. Follett, "Spy as Hero," 81.

14. Ibid., 75.

15. Follett, "Altar," 14; Hendrickson, "Winging Ways," 3.

16. Rubin, "Between C.I.A.," 9.

17. Macdonald, "Follett," 114; "Influences," 13.

18. MacLeish, "Finely Stitched," 4.

19. Follett, "Enchant," 29.

Chapter 5: Change and Adaptation

1. Bruce Merry, *Anatomy of the Spy Thriller* (Montreal: McGill, 1977), 50.

2. Follett, "Enchant," 11.

3. Baker, "PW Interviews," 55.

4. Andrew F. Macdonald, *Dictionary of Literary Biography,* 1989 ed., s.v. "Forsyth, Frederick"; Macdonald, "Follett," 117.

5. Roger Ebert, review of "The Day of the Locust" (Universal Pictures movie), in Baseline's *Encyclopedia of Film* (online), 10 Apr. 1996, 52 lines; Robert Bookbinder, *The Films of the Seventies* (New London, CT: Citadel Press, 1982), 87.

6. Rob Edelman, "Eye of the Needle," *Magill's Cinema Annual,* 1982, 150; David Ansen, "Spy on the Run," review of "Eye of the Needle" (United Artists movie), *Newsweek,* 3 Aug. 1981: 50.

7. André Bazin, *What Is Cinema?* trans. Hugh Grey (Berkeley: University of California Press, 1967), 68.

8. Macdonald, "Forsyth," 127; *Motion Picture Guide,* 1986 ed., s.v. "Day of the Jackal, The."

9. MacLeish, "Finely Stitched," 4; McDowell, "Focus," 102.

10. George Bluestone, *Novels into Film* (1957; reprint, Berkeley: University of California Press, 1966), viii.

11. Follett, "Enchant," 11.

12. Janet Maslin, "Love and Intrigue," review of "Eye of the Needle" (United Artists movie), *New York Times,* 24 July 1981, sec. 3: 10.

13. Rudolf Arnheim, *Film As Art* (1932; reprint, Berkeley: University of California Press, 1957), 217.

14. Edelman, "Eye," 150; *Motion Picture Guide,* 1986 ed., s.v. "Eye of the Needle."

15. Merry, *Anatomy,* 2.

16. Bookbinder, *Films,* 88; Ansen, "On the Run," 50.

17. Maslin, "Love," 10; Edelman, "Eye," 148.

18. McDowell, "Focus," 102.

19. Maslin, "Love," 10.

20. Joseph McBride, *Orson Welles* (New York: Viking, 1972), 141.

Chapter 6: Television as Interpretation

1. John Simon, *Movies into Films* (New York: Dial, 1971), 86; Francois Truffaut, *Hitchcock* (New York: Simon and Schuster, 1967), 128.

2. Arnheim, *Art,* 217.

3. Macdonald, "Follett," 113; Follett, "Enchant," 11.

4. Lauerman, "Novelist," 3; Kirchhoff, "Thriller Writer," 25.

5. Hendrickson, "Winging Ways," 1.

6. In 1980, the *Los Angeles Times* reported that Follett had completed a film treatment of *The Key to Rebecca* and that CBS had purchased *Triple* for a future TV mini-series. See Isenberg, "Thrillers," 5.

7. Stephanie Mansfield, "TV Preview: 'Rebecca,'" *Washington Post,* 1 May 1985, sec. 3: 1; Ray Loynd, review of "Lie Down with Lions" (Hannibal Films TV Movie), *Variety,* 6 June 1994: 30; John O'Connor, "TV and Movies Mingle," review of "Lie Down with Lions" (Hannibal Films TV Movie), *New York Times,* 14 June 1994, sec. 3: 20.

8. Isenberg, "Thrillers," 1; Andrews, "Three Stooges," 9.

9. Isenberg, "Thrillers," 5.

10. Robert Lekachman, "The Thriller Connection," review of *The Key to Rebecca, The Nation,* 20 Dec. 1980: 677; Andrews, "Three Stooges," 9; Busch, "Spy Story," 6.

11. Gareffa, "Follett," 189.

12. Ken Follett, *The Key to Rebecca* (New York: Morrow, 1980; reprint, New York: NAL Signet, 1980), 105. All subsequent quotations or page citations from *The Key to Rebecca* refer to the reprint edition.

13. Ross, "CA Interview," 152.

14. Busch, "Spy Story," 6.

15. Michael Kilian, "Hooked on Classics," interview with Douglas McGrath, et al., *Chicago Tribune,* 27 Apr. 1997, sec. 7: 7.

16. Horace Newcombe, "Towards a Television Aesthetic," *TV: The Most Popular Art* (New York: Anchor, 1974), 247-51.

17. Ibid., 249.

18. John Corry, "Cliff Robertson in 'The Key to Rebecca,' a Two-Part Movie," review of "The Key to Rebecca" (Taft Entertainment TV Movie), *New York Times,* 29 Apr. 1985: 3, 16; Mansfield, "TV Preview," 2.

19. Robert Richardson, *Literature and Film* (Bloomington: Indiana University Press, 1969), 53.

Other film versions of these stories also exist, with similar visual references. DeMille made his first version of "The Ten Commandments" in 1923 and a version of "Cleopatra" in 1934. DeMille's "The Sign of the Cross" (1932) includes the famous scene of Claudette Colbert bathing in milk. "Samson and Delilah" was re-made for television in 1984.

20. Mansfield, "TV Preview," 2.

21. Loynd, rev. of "Lie Down," 30; Janet Martineau, "Triple Threat Hinders 'Twins,'" review of "The Third Twin" (CBS TV Movie) *Saginaw News,* 8 Nov. 1997, sec. 4: 2.

22. Ken Follett, "Capitalism, Socialism and Radio Wawa," *The Bookseller,* 18 Sept. 1992: 826.

23. David Bianculli, *Teleliteracy: Taking Television Seriously* (New York: Continuum, 1992), 274, 141.

24. Newcombe, "Aesthetic," 256.

25. McDowell, 102.

Chapter 7: The Art of the First Chapter

1. Ross, "CA Interview," 151.

2. David Shaw, "Pre-WW I Thriller in Follett Footsteps," review of *The Man from St. Petersburg, Los Angeles Times Book Review,* 30 May 1982: 16.

3. Nancy Yates Hoffman, "A Novel Ahead of Its Time for All the Wrong Reasons," review of *Triple, Los Angeles Times,* 7 Oct. 1979, sec. 5: 4; Busch, "Spy Story," 6; John Coleman, "On New Crime Fiction," review of *Lie Down with Lions, Sunday Times* (London), 29 Dec. 1985: 42; Roderick MacLeish, "From Russia, with Love," review of *The Man from St. Petersburg, Book World: Washington Post,* 25 Apr. 1982: 3; Macdonald, "Follett," 120; Andrews, "Three Stooges," 9.

4. Andrews, "Three Stooges," 9.

5. Lauerman, "Novelist," 3.

6. Follett, *Paper Money,* iv.

7. Baker, "PW Interviews," 55.

The first chapter from *The Key to Rebecca* was published by *People Weekly* in 1980 and was entitled "Across the Sahara Towards Death and Intrigue." The opening of *Lie Down with Lions* appeared under that same title in *Cosmopolitan* in 1986. Sections from *Eye of the Needle* were published in *Cosmopolitan* in 1979. Rather than selecting a single chapter, however, the editors chose to condense the entire novel, which I believe is yet another indication of the overall artistic integrity and general superiority of that earlier work.

8. Judith Scherer Herz, *The Short Narratives of E. M. Forster* (New York: St. Martin's, 1988), 69.

9. Brander Matthews, *The Philosophy of the Short-Story* (New York: Longmans, 1901), 16.

10. Charles E. May, *Short Story Theories* (Athens: Ohio University Press, 1976): 5, 7.

11. Ian Hamilton, *In Search of J. D. Salinger* (New York: Random House, 1988): 62-63.

12. Gumbel, Interview, 24 Sept. 1991; Hamilton, *Salinger,* 63.

13. Hamilton, *Salinger,* 63.

14. Matthews, *Philosophy,* 15-16.

15. Since this is a novel, however, the dramatic question is reopened in the next chapter, but the issue and the ultimate resolution have already been stated definitively in the first chapter.

16. Mayer, "High Noon," 83; May, *Short Story,* 7.

17. Dickinson's "Because I Could Not Stop for Death" and Wordsworth's "Resolution and Independence," in particular.

18. The retention of both names in some editions of *The Key to Rebecca* is most likely a printer's oversight.

19. May, *Short Story,* 119.

20. Kostelanetz, qtd. in May, 217.

21. Ibid., 216.

22. Alberto Moravia, *Man As End: A Defense of Humanism* (New York: Farrar, Strauss, 1969), 182.

23. Edgar Allan Poe, "Review of Twice-Told Tales," *Graham's Magazine,* May 1842; reprinted in *The Heath Anthology of American Literature,* ed. Paul Lauter (Lexington, MA: Heath, 1994), 425.

24. Ken Follett, *Triple* (New York: Arbor House, 1979; reprint, New York: NAL Signet, 1979), 1. All subsequent quotations or page citations from *Triple* refer to the reprint edition.

25. Poe, rev. of *Twice,* 425. For a discussion of the structure of fairy tales, see Vladimir Propp's *The Morphology of the Folktale* (1927). Bruno Bettleheim's *The Uses of Enchantment: The Meaning and Importance of Fairy Tales* (1976) is the best-known psychoanalytical study of traditional stories.

26. Vladimir Propp, *The Morphology of the Folktale* (1927; reprint, Austin: University of Austin, 1968), 62.

27. Poe, rev. of *Twice,* 425.

Chapter 8: Unification and Evaporation

1. Laurence Behrens and Leonard Rosen, eds., "Passion in Print," *Reading for College Writers* (Boston: Little, Brown, 1987), 235-84. The chapter contains much useful information on the phenomenon of category romance novels, and reprints Silhouette and Harlequin guideline sheets, interviews with romance writers, and selections from novels.

2. Adams, "Follett," 203; Robert Lekachman, "Good Boys, Bad Boys," review of *Triple, The Nation,* 26 Apr. 1980: 505.

3. Janice Radway, *Reading the Romance* (Chapel Hill: University of North Carolina Press, 1984), 155.

4. Cawelti and Rosenberg, *Spy Story,* 219.

5. Dennis Hamilton, "The Mentor," *Espionage Magazine,* Feb. 1985: 105-18.

6. Tania Modleski, *Loving with a Vengeance* (New York: Methuen, 1982),

74, 61.

7. Graham Greene, *Collected Essays* (1969; reprint, Harmondsworth, England: Penguin, 1983), 167.

8. Buchan, *The 39 Steps,* 23; Jerry Palmer, *Thrillers: Genesis and Structure of a Popular Genre* (New York: St. Martin's, 1979), 87.

9. Ryall, *Hitchcock,* 120; Modleski, *Loving,* 17.

10. Radway, *Romance,* 131.

11. Graham Greene, *The Human Factor* (New York: Simon and Schuster, 1978).

12. Ken Follett, *The Man from St. Petersburg* (New York: Morrow, 1982; reprint, New York: NAL Signet, 1982). All subsequent quotations or page citations from *The Man from St. Petersburg* refer to the reprint edition.

13. Behrens and Rosen, eds., "Passion," 268; Radway, *Romance,* 132.

14. T. J. Binyon, "Raging Anarchy," review of *The Man from St. Petersburg, Times Literary Supplement,* 4 June 1982: 622.

15. Radway, *Romance,* 134.

16. Behrens and Rosen, eds., Harlequin Guidelines qtd. in "Passion," 266.

17. Julian Symons points to two traditions in the spy novel. The first is conservative and supportive of the status quo. The second is radical and critical of authority. *Bloody Murder: From the Detective Story to the Crime Novel: A History* (Harmondsworth, England: Penguin, 1974), 247.

18. Radway, *Romance,* 131.

19. Behrens and Rosen, eds., "Passion," 268.

20. Northrop Frye, *The Anatomy of Criticism* (Princeton: Princeton University Press, 1957), 107; Frederic Jameson, *The Political Unconscious: Narrative as Socially Symbolic Act* (Ithaca: Cornell University Press, 1981), 119.

21. Bruno Bettleheim, *The Uses of Enchantment* (New York: Vintage, 1977), 83.

22. Shaw, "Pre-WWI Thriller," 16; Bakerman, "Follett," 384.

23. Ken Follett, "The Abiding Heart," *Good Housekeeping,* Aug. 1990: 60-69.

Chapter 9: The Architecture of the Novel

1. Ross, "CA Interview," 152; Lauerman, "Novelist," 3; Fred Hauptfuhrer, "Out of the Pages," *People Weekly,* 25 Sept. 1978: 108.

2. Baker, "PW Interviews," 54; Hauptfuhrer, "Out of the Pages," 108; Ross, "CA Interview," 152.

3. Hauptfuhrer, "Out of the Pages," 108; Sybil Steinberg, "'The Pillars' of a New Success for Ken Follett and Morrow," *Publishers' Weekly,* 21 July 1989: 38-39.

4. Kirchhoff, "Thriller Writer," 25; Steinberg, "New Success," 38; *Current Biography,* 1990 ed.

5. *Bestsellers,* 1989 ed., s.v. "Follett, Ken."

6. Review of *The Pillars of the Earth, People Weekly,* 25 Dec. 1989: 27; "Interview: Ken Follett," *Ellery Queen's Mystery Magazine,* Dec. 1978: 96.

7. Lask, "Publishing," 26; *Current Biography,* 1990 ed.

8. Linnea Lannon, "Follett's 'Pillars' May Sell, but Writing Won't Stand Up," *Detroit Free Press,* 10 Sept. 1989, sec. 14: 7; Steinberg, "New Success," 38.

9. Cecilia Holland, "Spire Thriller," *New York Times,* 10 Sept. 1989: 41.

David Cowart, *History and the Contemporary Novel* (Carbondale: Southern Illinois University Press, 1989), has divided historical novels into four categories: those novels that strive above all for historical accuracy; works that reverse history to speculate on the future; fiction that dramatizes a turning point in history; and novels which project contemporary tensions onto the past. Cowart maintains that "the more multi-faceted the novel, the more likely it will manifest features from more than one category" (11).

Because of the interest in historical accuracy, *The Pillars of the Earth* would fit primarily under the first category, but in its concluding sections it focuses on a turning point in history, the murder of Thomas à Becket. Numerous reviewers have pointed to the contemporary psychology of Follett's characters or to their modern turns-of-phrase. Whether deliberately planned or an anachronistic lapse, the use of modern characters in costume places *The Pillars of the Earth* in the long tradition of the projection novel.

10. Ralph Novak, review of *The Pillars of the Earth, People Weekly,* 18 Sept. 1989: 37; Cynthia Johnson, "Fiction," *Library Journal,* July 1986: 108.

11. Compton Mackenzie, afterword to *Ivanhoe,* by Sir Walter Scott (New York: NAL Signet, 1962), 491-97.

12. Patrick Reardon, "Follett's Thriller Skills Adapt Well to History," *Chicago Tribune,* 10 Sept. 1989, sec. 14: 7.

13. Ken Follett, with René L. Maurice, *The Heist of the Century* (London: Fontana Books, 1978; reprinted as *Under the Streets of Nice* [New York, Arbor House, 1978]), 1. Quotations refer to the reprint edition.

14. Georg Lukács, *The Historical Novel,* trans. Hannah and Stanley Mitchell (Boston: Beacon Press, 1962), 214. See Gareffa, "Follett," 189.

15. Rhona Martin, *Writing Historical Fiction* (New York: St. Martin's, 1988), 9; Radway, *Romance,* 189.

16. Holland, "Spire Thriller," 41.

17. Ross, "CA Interview," 151.

18. Janet Burroway, *Writing Fiction* (Boston: Little-Brown, 1987), 8.

19. Bakerman, "Follett," 384.

20. Steinberg, "New Success," 38.

21. Ross, "CA Interview," 151.

Chapter 10: Politics and Historical Revisionism

1. Follett, "Enchant," 9.

2. Crampton, "Social," 10; Ross, "CA Interview," 151.

3. Marchand, "Magic Hand," 10.

4. Crampton, "Social," 11.

5. Candy and Denis Atherton, "Relative Values," *Sunday Times Magazine* (London), 1 May 1994: 13.

6. Lesley White, "The Lesley White Interview: Barbara Follett," *Sunday Times* (London), 7 Feb. 1993, sec. 2: 2; "Novelist Launches Scholarship," *Times* (London), 14 Jan. 1988: 12; Jacques, "Ken and Barbie," 50; Crampton, "Social," 9-10.

Costs in pounds have been converted to dollars using the exchange rate of the time: 1 UK = 1.6 US.

7. Jacques, "Ken and Barbie," 51; Crampton, "Social," 10; Marchand, "Magic Hand," 10.

8. Crampton, "Social," 10.

9. Follett, "Socialism," 828.

10. Jacques, "Ken and Barbie," 51; Erich Fromm, *Marx's Concept of Man* (New York: Ungar, 1961), vi, 5.

11. Crampton, "Social," 10.

12. Jacques, "Ken and Barbie," 51; Crampton, "Social," 10.

13. Crampton, "Social," 10.

14. Steinberg, "New Success," 39.

15. Irving Howe, *Politics and the Novel* (Cleveland: Meridian, 1957), 19. All subsequent quotations or page citations from *Politics and the Novel* refer to this edition.

16. Kate Saunders, "Goodies and Baddies," *Sunday Times* (London), 26 Sept. 1993, sec. 6: 13.

17. Patricia Altner, review of *A Place Called Freedom, Library Journal*, Aug. 1995: 115.

18. Jacques, "Ken and Barbie," 52.

19. Ibid.

20. Thomas Hines, "Victorian England Gets Real," review of *A Dangerous Fortune, Los Angeles Times,* 12 Dec. 1993, sec. 6: 8.

In Disraeli's work *Sybil* (1845; reprint, London: Oxford University Press, 1926), a character describes England as "Two nations; between whom there is no intercourse and no sympathy; who are as ignorant of each other's habits, thoughts, feelings, as if they were dwellers in different zones, or inhabitants of different planets; who are formed by a different breeding, are fed by different food, are ordered by different manners, and are not governed by the same laws . . . THE RICH AND THE POOR" (67). This two-word label was soon applied to many subsequent Victorian novels of social protest.

21. Chris Petrakos, "A Smorgasbord of Suspense," review of *A Place Called Freedom, Chicago Tribune,* 17 Sept. 1995, sec. 14: 6; Review of *A Dangerous Fortune, Publishers' Weekly,* 23 Aug. 1993: 57.

22. Review of *A Place Called Freedom, Publishers' Weekly,* 5 June 1995: 48-49.

23. Harriet Beecher Stowe, *Uncle Tom's Cabin* (1852; reprint, New York: Penguin, 1981), 506. All subsequent quotations or page citations from *Uncle Tom's Cabin* refer to the reprint edition.

24. Holland, "Spire Thriller," 41.

Saunders points out that such a characterization of professional people is particularly "[i]n line with new Labour philosophy" and the contemporary view that a person with money does not have to be vicious ("Goodies," 13). Follett himself defends the role of the self-made rich within a political group traditionally defined by its working-class membership: "A lot of people feel a mild distaste for the idea that if you give the Labour Party £1,000, you will get invited to three or four cocktail parties. . . . The bottom line is that trade union money is going to decline" (Crampton, "Social," 11).

25. Saunders, "Goodies," 6.

Aunt Augusta, as a member of the Victorian upper-middle class, would probably also have enjoyed a diet rich in meats. The inhabitants of London, men and women both, were described in 1854 as the greatest consumers of meat "in the world" who were justifiably proud of "that British beef which is the boast of John Bull." In E. Royston Pike, *Golden Times: Documents of the Victorian Age* (New York: Schocken, 1972), 58.

The abolition of fox-hunting is an avowed aim of the *contemporary* British Labour Party.

26. White, "Interview," 2; Lauerman, "Novelist," 3.

27. White, "Interview," 2.

28. In an earlier, less subtle work entitled *Amok: King of Legend* (London: Futura, 1976), Follett, writing as "Bernard L. Ross," described a group of wildlife photographers who also enter a lush green valley and who remark specifically that it resembles " 'The Garden of Eden' " (142). This suggests that religious iconography has long been present in his work, as has a nostalgia for paradise.

29. Robert Crampton, "Banking on a Capital Idea," *Times* (London), 9 July 1994, Weekend: 14.

30. Lauerman, "Novelist," 3.

Chapter 11: Conclusion

1. Chris Petrakos, "Secrets Spilled by a Spy Who Loves Music," review of thriller novels including *A Dangerous Fortune, Chicago Tribune,* 19 Sept. 1993, sec. 14: 7.

2. The ritual of dining becomes a central motif in social realist works. In John Braine's *Room at the Top,* Joe Lampton is queried by Susan Brown's father during a private dinner at the Conservative Club and nearly chokes on his "first spoonful of game soup" (206). Piers Roper, as was noted in chapter 3, "toyed with breast of turkey and green salad" while Monica eats hungrily and questions him (*SK* 82). Preston Berrington also "toyed with his salad" in *The Third Twin* and earlier had only been superficially in control while dining with Jeannie Ferrami (103). In *The Hammer of Eden,* "Judy ate with gusto" (242) and for the most part directs the conversation. When her dinner companion appears "troubled . . . she reached across the table and squeezed his hand" (242). In each instance, the setting allows for some examination of social structure but, more importantly, each scene demonstrates who is in control by the character's ease or discomfort while eating.

3. Ken Follett, "Author Transcripts," Barnes and Noble Online Web Site, 15 Dec. 1997, <http:www.barnesandnoble.com>.

4. Burroway, *Writing Fiction,* 223-24.

5. MacLeish, "Finely Stitched," 4.

6. James Moffett and Kenneth R. McElheny, *Points of View: An Anthology of Short Stories* (New York: NAL Mentor, 1966), 405.

7. Follett, "Spy as Hero," 75.

8. The image of the Englishman in exile is well established in 20th-century fiction, from Joseph Conrad's *Lord Jim* (1900) to Graham Greene's *The Quiet American* (1955). More recent manifestations of the type have appeared in Brian Moore's *The Luck of Ginger Coffey* (1960), Kingsley Amis' *One Fat Englishman* (1963), and Anthony Burgess' *Enderby's Dark Lady* (1984). These three novels are all set in North America.

9. Ken Follett, "Author Transcripts," Barnes and Noble Online Web Site, 2 Nov. 1998, <http:www.barnesandnoble.com>.

10. Ronald Seth, *Encyclopedia of Espionage* (Garden City, NY: Doubleday, 1974); Christopher Dobson and Ronald Payne, *The Dictionary of Espionage* (London: Harrap, 1984).

11. Gumbel, Interview, 24 Sept. 1991.

12. Lawrence Donegan, "Author Claims Unknown Writer 'Stole' War Plot," *Guardian* (London), 16 Sept. 1996, sec. 1: 5.

13. "Influences," 13.

14. Rubins, "Between C.I.A.," 9.

BIBLIOGRAPHY

Works by Ken Follett

The Big Needle. [Symon Myles, pseud.] London: Everest Books, 1974. Reprinted under name Ken Follett, New York: Zebra, 1979.

The Big Black. [Symon Myles, pseud.] London: Everest, 1974.

The Big Hit. [Symon Myles, pseud.] London: Everest, 1975.

The Shakeout. London: Harwood-Smart, 1975. Reprint, New York: Armchair Detective, 1990.

The Bear Raid. London: Harwood-Smart, 1976. Reprint, New York: Armchair Detective, 1990.

The Secret of Kellerman's Studio. London: Abelard, 1976. Reprinted under name Ken Follett, New York: Morrow Junior Books, 1990.

The Power Twins and the Worm Puzzle. [Martin Martinsen, pseud.] London: Abelard, 1976. Reprinted under name Ken Follett, New York: Morrow Junior Books, 1990.

Amok: King of Legend. [Bernard L. Ross, pseud.] London: Futura, 1976.

The Modigliani Scandal. [Zachary Stone, pseud.] London: Collins, 1976. Reprinted under name Ken Follett, New York: NAL Signet, 1985.

Paper Money. [Zachary Stone, pseud.] London: Collins, 1977. Reprinted under name Ken Follett, New York: NAL Signet, 1987.

Capricorn One. [Bernard L. Ross, pseud.] London: Futura, 1978.

Eye of the Needle. (Published in England as *Storm Island.*) Macdonald and Janes, 1978. Reprint, New York: Arbor House, 1978.

The Heist of the Century. (With René Louis Maurice.) London: Fontana Books, 1978. Reprinted as *Under the Streets of Nice: The Bank Heist of the Century.* Bethesda, MD: National Press, 1986.

"Books That Enchant and Entertain." *The Writer* June 1979: 9-11.

Triple. Arbor House, 1979. Reprint, New York: NAL Signet, 1979.

The Key to Rebecca. New York: Morrow, 1980. Reprint, New York: NAL Signet, 1980.

The Man from St. Petersburg. New York: Morrow, 1982. Reprint, New York: NAL Signet, 1982.

"The Spy as Hero and Villain." *The Murder Mystique: Crime Writers on Their Art.* Ed. Lucy Freeman. New York: Frederick Ungar, 1982.

On Wings of Eagles. New York: Morrow, 1983. Reprint, New York: NAL Signet, 1984.

"On the Altar of Overlord." Review of *Fall from Grace* by Larry Collins. *New York Times* 16 June 1985: 14.

Lie Down with Lions. London: Hamilton, 1985. Reprint, New York: NAL Signet, 1986.

"Model Rules for Socialists Under Cover." *New Statesman* 10 Apr. 1987: 8-10.

The Pillars of the Earth. New York: Morrow, 1989. Reprint, New York: NAL Signet, 1989.

"The Abiding Heart." *Good Housekeeping*. Aug. 1990: 60-69.

Night Over Water. New York: Morrow, 1991. Reprint, New York: NAL Signet, 1992.

"Capitalism, Socialism and Radio Wawa." *The Bookseller* 18 Sept. 1992: 826-29.

A Dangerous Fortune. New York: Morrow, 1993. Reprint, New York: Dell, 1993.

A Place Called Freedom. New York: Crown, 1995. Reprint, New York: Fawcett Crest, 1995.

The Third Twin. New York: Crown, 1996. Reprint, New York: Fawcett Crest, 1997.

The Hammer of Eden. New York: Crown, 1998.

INDEX